More Praise for *Women Lead the Way*

"If you, like me, have ever felt a door closing—in your family, at work, or in your community—just because you are female, then you know intuitively the depth of power that Linda Tarr-Whelan is intent on unleashing to change the world. This mission is urgent—our nation and the world require diverse and collaborative leadership now—and we'll get there only if you step up. Read this book!"

—*Sara K. Gould, President and CEO, Ms. Foundation for Women*

"Linda's focus on looking at what unites women is both refreshing and a hallmark of her own leadership. You will learn how the agenda that comes forward—more attention to children, education, entrepreneurship, health care, and balancing work and family—is the hidden story of new directions for the country. This book will give you the facts and the tips we all need to have more women lead the way."

—*Celinda Lake, President, Lake Research Partners*

"A compelling examination of what it takes to be a leader—from style to skill. Linda Tarr-Whelan offers an urgent call to action for women in this country, both intimate and tough in its historical assessment, sometimes didactic, often inspiring, and always important. By drawing on her rich and diverse journey in politics and policy, she makes a powerful case that women must become 'change agents' and join the ranks of leadership in every part of our society."

—*U.S. Representative Rosa L. DeLauro*

"This book's central idea is as simple as it is profound: when women are better represented in decision-making bodies, organizations and institutions produce better results—both for their constituents and for society as a whole. It isn't about what's wrong with the world or what's holding women back. Instead, Tarr-Whelan has written a 'how-to' manual, offering practical ideas for how women leaders can transform institutions and change the world."

—*Joe Keefe, President and CEO, Pax World Management Corporation*

"The super-savvy Linda Tarr-Whelan draws on her many impressive achievements to show us how more women can make it to the top in government and in the private sector. We ignore her at our peril. Only when women become truly equal partners in this country's decision making will we realize our full promise as a beacon to all the world."

—*Ellen Chesler, PhD, Director, Eleanor Roosevelt Initiative at the Roosevelt House Public Policy Institute at Hunter College, the City University of New York and author of* Woman of Valor: Margaret Sanger and the Birth Control Movement

"Linda Tarr-Whelan uses her lifetime of rich and varied experiences to lay out a plan for empowering women in both the public and private sectors. She offers women an important road map to leadership in government and business. This timely book takes up the critical issue of the difference women in leadership make and how to maximize that difference."

—*Debbie Walsh, Director, Center for American Women and Politics, Eagleton Institute of Politics, Rutgers University*

"A must-read for this particular time in the history of women's leadership. There is a window of opportunity open for women's leadership here and now that compels all of us, women and men, to throw the window open wide and create the social change needed to rebalance the globe. Here is the guidebook for that work. Read, share, and act; it will make a world of difference."

—*Chris Grumm, President and CEO, Women's Funding Network*

"Linda's ability to translate macro issues into concrete action for executives, mothers, or some of us in need of informed inspiration is extraordinary. Whatever your passion or purpose is, she offers a road map that taps the wisdom of generations before us, as well as the hopes and potential of our daughters and sons. As you read, dream big and take your next step. Others will follow."

—*Anne B. Mosle, Vice President for Programs, W.K. Kellogg Foundation*

"Like Girl Scouting, which inspires girls of courage, confidence, and character, Tarr-Whelan's book builds on the idea of a sisterhood of female leaders, lifting and inspiring each other to do good works. *Women Lead the Way* calls on women to interact with purpose, to build a network of dynamic leaders who initiate progress."

—*Lidia Soto-Harmon, Deputy Executive Director, Girl Scout Council of the Nation's Capital*

"Linda Tarr-Whelan brings an extraordinary depth and breadth of personal experience—ranging from the nursing profession to a U.S. ambassadorship—to the issue of transformational leadership. Her wise counsel to women of all ages rings true, for those beginning to tackle the leadership challenge to those already making their mark. Read this to begin pursuing your passion."
—*Gail A. Raiman, Vice President, Public Affairs,*
Associated Builders and Contractors

"*Women Lead the Way* is a powerful reminder for those of us who have broken through and serve in leadership positions of the value that results from balanced decision making and the responsibilities we as individuals have in ensuring such balance occurs. Armed with data, a convincing case statement, knowledge of the obstacles still to be faced, and specific steps to overcome them, Ms. Tarr-Whelan has provided women a clear path forward."
—*Myrl Weinberg, President, National Health Council*

"Linda Tarr-Whelan brilliantly depicts the *passion* of women's leadership with the *power* that fuels it. Her words inspire, motivate, and challenge us to embrace our unique *woman-perspective* in the corporate, civic, and political arenas so that we collectively bring about the global transformation that is only possible when we do so."
—*Molly Barker, Founder and Vision Keeper, Girls on the Run*

"A game-changing book from one of the most fascinating and articulate spokeswomen of our time. Linda Tarr-Whelan has been our North Star, constantly challenging us to think beyond convention so we may find a better way to lead down a path less traveled. She not only inspires us to think entrepreneurially about the possibilities but, like the great leader she is, she provides us the tools to do our work."
—*Amy Millman, President, Springboard Enterprises*

"Through thought-provoking statistics and stories, *Women Lead the Way* candidly holds a mirror to our costly gender and power reality. Linda acts as a personal mentor to help women in all walks of life take practical steps to gain expertise, exposure, and experience and find their place as leaders. Every man should read this book to learn about the profit from 'womenomics' and the too-often-hidden value in women's thoughts, hearts, and ways of seeing the world."
—*Megan White, Founder and President, ZanaAfrica, Kenya*

"A breakthrough book that for the first time brings together the lessons of personal, community, national, and international experience in leading programs for women's equity. It is inspirational, rich in ideas and examples, and a practical road map for men and women wanting to step forward to lead deep change for stronger societies."

—*Elizabeth McAllister, strategic management consultant,*
former Canadian government official specializing in
women's development, and World Bank senior executive

"Tarr-Whelan makes a compelling case for gender balance in the boardroom and under the Capitol dome as the gateway to a better future for our society. Her step-by-step guidance on the pathway to transformational leadership instructs and inspires readers on 'being the change we seek to make.' Reading this book should be a priority for women change-makers!

—*Georgia State Senator Nan Grogan Orrock,*
President, Women Legislators' Lobby of WAND

"Linda Tarr-Whelan is not only a change agent; she is a true force of nature. What is powerful and awe inspiring about Linda's book is that it is a highly achievable call to action! *Women Lead the Way* is a brilliant achievement! If you want a better world, her voice on the issue of empowering women is nothing short of amazing and will send you on your way."

—*Janet Hanson, Founder and CEO, 85 Broads*

"As the president of a women's college that puts a priority on the development of leadership skills, I found *Women Lead the Way* to be an impressive collection of strategies and tools for women who want to make a difference in the communities in which they live. Linda Tarr-Whelan's combination of personal stories and hard research makes for a persuasive guide to the creation of the kind of balanced leadership that we need to meet the challenges of the 21st century."

—*Janet L. Holmgren, President, Mills College*

WOMEN LEAD THE WAY

To Meg —
With best wishes for a great
future
Linda Tarr-Whelan

WOMEN LEAD THE WAY

Your Guide to Stepping Up to Leadership and Changing the World

Linda Tarr-Whelan

BK

Berrett–Koehler Publishers, Inc.
San Francisco
a BK Currents book

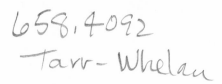

658.4092
Tarr-Whelan

Berrett-Koehler Publishers, Inc.
235 Montgomery Street, Suite 650
San Francisco, CA 94104-2916
Tel: (415) 288-0260 Fax: (415) 362-2512 www.bkconnection.com

ORDERING INFORMATION

Quantity sales. Special discounts are available on quantity purchases by corporations, associations, and others. For details, contact the "Special Sales Department" at the Berrett-Koehler address above.

Individual sales. Berrett-Koehler publications are available through most bookstores. They can also be ordered directly from Berrett-Koehler: Tel: (800) 929-2929; Fax: (802) 864-7626; www.bkconnection.com

Orders for college textbook/course adoption use. Please contact Berrett-Koehler: Tel: (800) 929-2929; Fax: (802) 864-7626.

Orders by U.S. trade bookstores and wholesalers. Please contact Ingram Publisher Services, Tel: (800) 509-4887; Fax: (800) 838-1149; E-mail: customer.service@ingram publisherservices.com; or visit www.ingrampublisherservices.com/Ordering for details about electronic ordering.

Berrett-Koehler and the BK logo are registered trademarks of Berrett-Koehler Publishers, Inc.

Printed in the United States of America

Berrett-Koehler books are printed on long-lasting acid-free paper. When it is available, we choose paper that has been manufactured by environmentally responsible processes. These may include using trees grown in sustainable forests, incorporating recycled paper, minimizing chlorine in bleaching, or recycling the energy produced at the paper mill.

Library of Congress Cataloging-in-Publication Data

Tarr-Whelan, Linda.
  Women lead the way : your guide to stepping up to leadership and changing the world / Linda Tarr-Whelan. — 1st ed.
     p. cm.
  Includes bibliographical references and index.
  ISBN 978-1-60509-135-8 (hardcover : alk. paper)
  1. Women executives. 2. Organizational change. I. Title.
  HD6054.3.T37 2009
  658.4'092082—dc22   2009021826

FIRST EDITION

14 13 12 11 10 09   10 9 8 7 6 5 4 3 2 1

Copyeditor: Lynn Golbetz
Production, interior design, and composition: Leigh McLellan Design

Contents

This book is dedicated to a better future for
Harper Jane, Isabella, Gehrig, and Cale
With appreciation for their love to
Melinda, Scott, and Emily
and
With my love always to Keith

Foreword

Marie Wilson, *Founder and President, The White House Project*

Picture this: A problem of vital importance emerges in your community, and you are asked to gather a team you deem essential to its solution. Then you are told you can't use half of the collected intelligence. That is basically the problem we face in politics and boardrooms across America—we systemically neglect one of our nation's most vital resources: women.

Women are more than half of the U.S. population, yet we still occupy between 16% and 20% of the leadership positions across major sectors of society. Research consistently shows that when women lead side by side with men, more alternatives are offered, more skill sets are used, and more out-of-the-box thinking occurs from both genders. Linda Tarr-Whelan, in *Women Lead the Way: Your Guide to Stepping Up to Leadership and Changing the World,* understands this resource crisis from decades of observation and personal experience, and she wants women like you (and those you know) to solve it, once and for all.

Linda's "30% Solution" advocates for truly balanced leadership, with women holding at least 30% of the seats at any power table. This percentage keeps the focus off gender and on the agenda. It is this critical mass of numbers, as I too have preached through the years, which will create a more productive work environment, a revitalized society, increased economic growth, and reinvigorated democratic participation.

What most people don't know (Americans often think women already run the world) is that we fall further behind every year. When I started The White House Project a decade ago to bring more women into leadership across sectors, our country was thirty-seventh in the world in women's political participation. We are now a pathetic sixty-ninth. Norway, as an example, is far ahead of us; that country passed a law requiring that publicly traded companies have at least 40% women on their boards, and if these firms failed to do so by the deadline, they were fined. Guess what? They met the deadline. Corporate boards in the United States, by comparison, are 17% female, with no structural change on tap to alter that.

Women Lead the Way is an optimistic book focused on adding women's strengths to decision making precisely at a time when these very strengths are most required. Collaboration, consensus building, a focus on relationships and partnerships, and a deep commitment to both family and work are badly needed; women are known to consistently bring these values to the table. Linda builds the case for balanced leadership based on credible business and political data from around the globe, showing clearly the bottom-line benefits. Women are catalysts for change, but the results are a win-win for everyone.

My book, *Closing the Leadership Gap: Why Women Can and Must Help Run the World,* like Linda's, deals with the importance of women's leadership and the cultural challenges to it before we can be fully accepted. Linda's inspiring and engaging work adds compelling research, international experience, and personal stories, and then provides you with practical tips to help you climb the ladder and wedge the door open for other women to follow. As the old spiritual says, "Lift as you rise."

Linda and I have been professional colleagues and friends for twenty years. We found ourselves in national leadership positions in the '80s when I became president of the Ms. Foundation for Women and Linda was president of the Center for Policy Alternatives. With unusual career paths, both of us were somewhat unlikely candidates for these jobs. We began to collaborate on breakthrough projects and to share stories of our dreams and our children.

The book is packed with personal insights from Linda's long, fruitful career as an ambassador, nurse, union organizer, policy expert, business-woman, and consultant. Her diverse career allows her to dispel the myths and stereotypes that stand in our way, and to build confidence as you move toward bigger dreams.

Linda's dream, and mine, is having more and more women realize the world needs them in leadership. Research by The White House Project and so many other organizations supports the knowledge that Americans are comfortable with women leaders in the majority of sectors, and they even see women as better at most aspects of leadership. Take confidence in these findings as you explore the possibilities in your own life.

Finally, don't miss this book's "how to" strategies, straight from a woman who's been there and done that. Give this book to yourself or to another woman you think should be a leader. And make sure the men in your life read it, too, so they clearly see the advantages to them, their companies, and the country when more smart, savvy women are seated in their rightful spots at the tables of power.

The Story behind the Book

This book is the result of my personal leadership journey over more than four decades, much of it devoted to advancing and empowering women. I started writing the book with the belief that having more women leaders can make a big difference. Working on it for the past two years has convinced me more than ever that this is true. New leaders—women leaders— are needed to bring fresh air and creative ideas to meet the challenges of dramatic shifts in the world economy, communities, and companies.

Wherever decisions are made, you and women like you as leaders will add value and balance. As the humanitarian organization CARE says, "Women are the most underutilized natural resource in the world." As women, we bring great strength, talent, and experience but are underused as leaders. Here you will find a practical guide to make it easier for you and other women to confidently step up and be the transformational leaders we need in the numbers needed to modernize and improve outmoded ways of doing business while wedging the door open for more women.

Living a Change Agent Life

My quest started a long time ago on the first day of my first job as a registered nurse in the old days, when nurses wore a starched uniform and an organdy cupcake nurse's cap. The first day didn't go well for me. I was summarily fired. Why? I hadn't stood up when a male doctor came into the room. It didn't make any difference to the nursing director whether I was taking care of a patient's needs or not. Over the years I learned the ropes in quite different settings and met dynamic women wherever my career took me. After eight years as a nurse, I moved to grassroots organizing; to state government; to national policy positions in unions, as a think-tank CEO and senior fellow, in the White House, and as an ambassador; and then in the private sector as an international management consultant in a business partnership with my husband. Like most women, I have had a full life including more than a career. Being a wife and mother, a daughter (and daughter-in-law), a sister, and a grandmother have all given me great pleasure. Family life and surviving cancer have deepened and broadened my sense of the importance of living an integrated life with many layers, not simply a work-centric one.

The common thread in my life is being a change agent. I seem to have a constitutional unwillingness to accept the status quo when it seems unfair and a determination to try to find a better way. My family background began the process: my father was a national union leader and especially talented as a communicator. As children, my brother and I were taught our responsibility was to leave the world a bit better, a bit more just. Lots of problems need solutions, but over and over, in each of my career incarnations, I've been drawn to the cause of women's advancement and empowerment.

I've often wondered why this was the case. My best guess is this: I've seen the courage, energy, tenacity, determination, and sheer talent of women both as individuals and as friends and colleagues working together to improve the status quo. At the same time I've had a nagging aversion to repeatedly seeing such talented people take a backseat to someone else, just because of gender. I've witnessed women's creativity and energy bottled up by unproductive thinking and practices, and at the same time I've seen an unfulfilled need for better leadership.

One of the big lessons of my career has been this: who makes the decisions matters. Changing who decides changes what is decided. I started to watch carefully how very slowly women were moving up into decision-making positions. The top layer of politics and business remains much the same as it was generations ago.

Women have made great progress in many areas, but changing the agenda has been elusive. Despite all the hard work on important issues that have been at the top of women's to-do lists for decades—issues like family leave and economic security, early care and education for young children, and equal pay—little has changed. To me—and most women—these are necessities for an acceptable quality of life for American families. As you know from your own experience, they remain out of reach. Our daughter and other women of her generation are dealing with many of the same problems I faced as a single mom when our children were young.

I kept expecting more women to break through and bring their talents and vision to making the big decisions. In 1995, as a U.S. delegate to a United Nations world conference on women in China, I heard exciting ideas. For the first time I heard national leaders from all corners of the globe—mostly men—talk about the positive differences it makes for their entire societies when women are fully empowered to lead along with men. They focused on how change accelerated with one-third women at the table. The tipping point was not one or even two women in decision-making groups but what I introduce in the book as the 30% Solution. In the United States, though, there was silence: no public debate on why more balanced leadership was better, and very little action to reach the goal.

So I took matters into my own hands and began to work on this book. My goal is to see you—my reader—seated at one of those power tables and wedging the door open for more and more women to join you. We have much to do. Balanced leadership with a critical mass of women—that 30% Solution—will lead to different outcomes that are better for you, for us, for everyone.

Women Lead the Way
Will Help You Be a Transformational Leader

When we look at where we are now, I am reminded of the little but demanding voices from the backseat on family road trips, asking, "Are we there yet?" The statistics show we are not even close to the tipping point in most places. Statistics are important, but I wanted to know what women think about where we are. In a series of twelve informal focus groups across the country,[1] women across the board told me we are only halfway to tapping women's full talents. Almost without exception, early in these conversations a woman would say, "Our potential remains untapped," and others around the table would agree. Women I met share the belief underlying all the statistics. We have much more to offer.

I have seen the talent and commitment of women in worlds very different from my own and learned about the important, but often unrecognized, difference women make. Women's many-layered lives—mine and those of the women I have spoken with across this country—have a seamless character. Women see the significance of being both caregivers and effective and responsible economic and public actors. The world doesn't work this way now, but this perspective helps show us what solutions are needed.

This practical guide is my response to make it easier and smoother for you to be a transformational leader and affect the outcomes when issues are decided. As you—my reader—take your seat at power tables, you can create a ripple effect by bringing other qualified women along to join you. The spreading ripples will create opportunities for more and more women. When you take action, we all move forward.

This book gets you started on a women-led strategy to make positive change—working with like-minded men—to close the leadership gap and add our solutions. The idea is a simple one: Leadership balance brings greater progress. It is good for you, helps level the playing field for the women and girls who come behind you, and brings needed societal change. To help us get further, I've brought you some of the stories from women I've met along the way as well as from my own journey as a change agent. The stories and resources will introduce you to ideas that have the potential to change where you work, your community, and the wider society to reflect our values and vision.

Women Lead the Way Will Guide Your Journey

You will find a road map and tested tools here. The win-win plan can help you climb the ladder—whatever your field—and bring your passion, brains, and background to those offices where decisions are made. Strategic guidance will help you build energy and momentum by working together with others. You will have the business case, research data, how-to tips, and stories. Each chapter includes a "Takeaways" section or a quiz for you to assess where you are and a box called "This Week I Will. . ." to give you immediate action steps to get started. More resources are at the end of the book.

The Introduction: More Women Leaders, Better Leadership gives you the basics on becoming one of the new leaders we need and explains why it matters for a busy woman like you to engage. The bottom-line importance of balanced leadership reached through the 30% Solution is explained. You will discover how an Inside-Outside strategy of women Insiders at power tables working with Outsider advocates can create movement on long-stalled priorities.

I've written the book in two major sections. Part I: Women Lead the Way starts you off on your journey with the facts you need. Part II: Stepping Up to Leadership provides the tools you need as one woman, and we need as women together, to maximize our leadership potential. Resources follow the text to help you find additional information.

Part I: Women Lead the Way

Chapter 1: The 30% Solution explores how this proven and realistic catalyst for a wave of change works. Having at least one-third women making decisions has powerful positive outcomes, while having only one or a few women won't have the same effect. You will see why and how this concept brings about positive bottom-line results in contrast to current practice.

While the 30% Solution is practical and workable, some hurdles remain to getting there. Chapter 2: Modern Myths and Stereotypes confronts and dispels overhanging and self-reinforcing negative social and cultural attitudes. Chapter 3: The Everywoman Quiz gives you and your friends a way to check out real-world progress on women's leadership.

As women, we sometimes have preconceptions that gain the strength of myths and can cloud our recognition of systemic barriers to be addressed. Chapter 4: Breaking out of the Box gives you an opportunity to assess your Personal Confidence Factor, to face up to some "double-bind dilemmas" women find on the way up, and to resist personalization.

Hope is on the horizon. Chapter 5: Today's Transformational Leader helps you confidently promote and embody the leadership attributes, styles, and skills that fit many women naturally and are needed to meet the future head-on. Leaving old, outdated leadership models behind will strengthen your resolve.

Part II: Stepping Up to Leadership

The first practical tool is presented in Chapter 6: Starting Right Here, Right Now. Learn from the experience of other women and start where you are to make a difference every day. You can meet the leadership challenge with confidence knowing that change starts with the Power of One.

Chapter 7: Making Women's Power Visible presents the second tool, helping you create a buzz by highlighting women's differences and strengths as employees, customers, or clients. This changes the dynamics of determining the problems to be addressed and who can best solve them.

We move on to the next step in Chapter 8: Lifting as We Climb. You will learn more about how reaching a hand out to help other women and girls starts a chain reaction and increases your own leadership capacity and energy. When we join together, the effect doubles.

Next we take up how to magnify this approach. Chapter 9: Wedging the Door Open gives you an amazingly easy technique that really works to fast-track change in existing practices. The "women in every pool" plan makes sure least one woman is a finalist for every opening to accelerate progress.

Chapter 10: Together, We Rise puts all of this together by helping you strengthen your networks to give you the undergirding of support and mentoring every leader needs. Shared action through networking by starting small and continuing to widen the circle of impact and sustenance brings you—and all of us—further.

Now is the time to dream a little about where we should be in 2020—one hundred years after women won the right to vote. What will our legacy be when the glass ceiling has smashed to the ground and women are full partners with men in determining our destiny? The Conclusion: Dreaming Bigger Dreams challenges you and all of us to act as transformational leaders and change the world.

A Personal Note to My Readers

I hope the women you meet in this book will inspire you as they have inspired me. Beyond that, I trust you will be motivated to try some of the tools in this book to help you advance in your own leadership and be sure more and more other women have an opportunity to be leaders, too. The potential of balanced leadership is tremendous. Companies, communities, and this country can't afford to continue to pass up the full utilization of one of our greatest natural resources—women. You and other women and like-minded men can lead us to a different future by making sure we don't.

—Linda Tarr-Whelan
July 2009

Introduction
More Women Leaders, Better Leadership

On my desk is a campaign button reading, "Women will make the difference." I've had it since 1984, when Geraldine Ferraro was the first woman vice presidential candidate. And I'm sure it's right. Women have already made a huge difference as a force for change, and we continue to make critical contributions just about everywhere. Women's efforts have been invaluable, even though we have often been invisible.

There is one crucial place, however, where our talent is still largely untapped: the power tables where the course for the future is charted. A robust out-front role in setting priorities and allocating resources wherever the tough choices are made is essential to maximizing the contributions women can make. Some of us have been complacent, assuming women are naturally moving up to take our seats around the power tables. The reality is that we have a long way left to go.

A Compelling Need for New Thinking

In 2009, when *Women Lead the Way* went to press, a severe economic crisis gripped the United States and countries across the globe. Experts dissected the causes as whole industries collapsed. The leaders of major banks, corporations, and entire sectors of the economy were called to task. One very important factor became evident: Virtually none of the captains of industry were women. Women were not the leaders who had made the bad decisions that led, or at least added, to our economic miseries. Nicholas Kristof, columnist for the *New York Times*, asked, "Would we be in the same mess if Lehman Brothers [an investment house that failed] was Lehman Brothers and Sisters?"[1] My answer is, "Probably not."

To take another example, if the nation of Rwanda had had balanced leadership, would it have descended into the terrible genocide of 1994? We'll never know for sure, but we can make an educated guess: Rwanda now has a majority of women leaders, and it is a transformed nation.

Changing the Deciders Changes the Decisions

Tough economic times, dramatically shifting world events, unmet needs in the country—all call for looking beyond the current composition of leadership for different answers. To achieve sustainable long-term economic growth and well-being, leadership must become more balanced—and that means it must include more women.

Women's full participation in leadership improves outcomes. This is seemingly a well-kept secret in this country, although numerous books and studies have been published on it.[2] Extensive international experience in politics and current business and political research tell a powerful story of the correlation between balanced leadership and better results. When women (that means you!) step into leadership roles, you make life better—for yourself, your company or organization, and global society. *Women Lead the Way* shows how and why balanced leadership matters and helps you be part of creating a different future, one with enough women at the top to have a positive impact. We must move beyond having women appear "one-at-a-time performers," as identified by Supreme Court Justice Ruth Bader Ginsburg when she spoke in the Rose Garden next to President Bill Clinton, who had just appointed her to the Court.[3]

The 30% Solution

A sprinkling of women at the top, however inspirational, is not enough to change how companies or governments operate. The weight of cultural inertia is too great. But when that sprinkling grows until the leadership group is about one-third women, important things happen. Different decisions are made, and the move toward true parity in leadership gains momentum. If we can get to at least 30% women as partners at the power tables, we have a chance to change the world. I call this the 30% Solution.

Why 30%? This has proved to be the critical mass in any group of decision makers, the tipping point at which women's voices resonate fully to add the affirmative difference of our experiences and values. When your ideas, solutions, and approaches and those of other women are amplified enough to be heard and heeded, different options become possible. Customary and often outmoded or even counterproductive ways of doing business can be replaced by fresh ideas. Few women in top positions are likely to argue, "We've always done it this way." And with enough women in the mix, the hypercompetitiveness seemingly rampant in a homogeneous leadership structure is leavened.

With just a token woman or two at the table, the added strengths we bring simply don't carry the day. Lone women often feel like "fish out of water" or feel they must "go along to get along." A small number of women certainly can and do make a difference by bringing more women into power. Indeed, having even a few women at power tables as role models is vital. However, it is seldom enough to change outcomes. It is tough for one or a few women to lead the way on solving nagging problems, especially anything labeled a "women's issue," such as the need for family-friendly workplaces. More women are needed to gain the advantage of what law professor Deborah Rhode has called "the difference [that] 'difference' makes."[4]

On the other end of the spectrum, while true parity in leadership—50% women—is an ultimate goal mirroring society, 30% is where real change begins to happen. Also, parity becomes easier to accomplish after the tipping point is reached, because women can change long-standing practices to create more opportunity for others who come behind them. The 30% Solution acts as a floor for women moving up, not a ceiling.

Sometimes the best ideas are hidden in plain view. More than thirty years ago, Harvard Business School Professor Rosabeth Moss Kanter[5] first identified the importance of having a critical mass of about one-third women in corporate decision-making roles to positively affect outcomes. Regardless of the strategic importance of these findings, little attention was paid to the idea until 1995, when it gained prominence on the international stage. That year, almost two hundred nations attending a United Nations conference agreed on a goal of at least 30% women in decision making. These countries saw a need to establish genuine partnerships to determine their destinies. Since then more than one hundred nations have embarked on modernizing their leadership composition in line with the 30% Solution. Country after country has moved away from the historical model of totally or mostly male leadership to actively balance the scales with more women. The experiences that have validated their decisions are included throughout *Women Lead the Way*.

The 30% Solution is good business as well as smart politics. Catalyst, an independent research organization with deep ties to Fortune 500 companies, has undertaken a long line of important studies about the impact of having more women at the top. The findings build a strong case for predicting outcomes. Firms with one-third or more women as corporate officers and directors reap rich rewards: higher financial performance and better bottom lines, as well as more opportunity for upward mobility and improved policies for women and families. Best-practice companies (which are unfortunately few in number) are following a women-friendly model of leadership development as part of their business plan for success.

I haven't found studies about the 30% Solution in the nonprofit sector. Based on personal experience with the CEOs and boards of directors of a wide range of foundations and organizations, I would expect that these groups too would do better with balanced leadership. This is an area for more research.

Progress around the World, Paralysis at Home

The many countries working toward balanced leadership seem to realize that they can't afford to underutilize half their population. They see that moving ahead will take all the talent, energy, and ingenuity they have available. Old customs and ways of doing business that artificially limit the pool of potential leaders are increasingly seen as shortsighted. The men who run countries and companies have come to realize that having enough women at the top to speak up and be heard produces better results. It is not a zero-sum game of women vs. men or a discussion of rights. Instead, balanced leadership is a route to improving democracy and competitiveness.

The United States is used to leading the world in gender equality and women's advancement, but it no longer does. Other countries that started considerably behind the United States on this front are now moving faster. Despite the growing body of evidence supporting more diverse leadership, and despite major problems signaling a clear need to do things differently, changes in the status quo to reflect women's shared values and experience have been slow in coming to this country. In fact, as you will see in later chapters, progress toward balanced leadership has essentially stalled. Women are seldom playing a big role in determining what problems are critical enough to be solved or in suggesting different ways of doing things.

Women as a group, the "we" of this book, have certainly not stood idly by. Women have moved forward in impressive numbers to get further education, start businesses, lead community groups, raise families, advocate for change, and go to work. Over the years I have met incredible, dynamic women in every walk of life and at every level. Women are ready to fill new roles as the major talent pipeline for the future. Yet many more educated, experienced, qualified, savvy, and smart women are poised to lead than we find at the top rungs of career ladders.

In fact, the composition of the groups of people with the authority and power to define the landscape of problems and solutions in universities, law firms, major companies, and legislatures hasn't changed much overall. The higher up you go, the more men and fewer women are creating strategic plans to address problems. Even in the nonprofit world, where a vast number of women are at the top, the bigger the organization, the more likely it is to be run by men. In all too many places, women's opinions and expertise are not sought. Women's accomplishments are not on show. Times have changed, and so have women—but the paradigm of who leads remains virtually the same. Although it is seldom discussed in the United States, the 30% Solution can help.

History confirms the power of women as a force for change when we lead the way and are joined in the effort by like-minded men. Courageous women have seen problems in our society and acted. To cite only a few examples, women's leadership ended child labor and changed the law to protect girls and women from abuse and violence. Women sought and won the right to vote and the opportunities to go to school, participate in sports, work without sexual harassment, and gain credit in their own names. Taking the next steps to make the world a better place will require closing the leadership gap.

What Women Share

Like men, women are diverse in political position, occupation, age, family relationships, race, ethnicity, and economic status. However, women have found ways to cross these fault lines, share experiences, and act to improve our society. While much is made of the differences between and among women, these are definitely not the whole story.

I learned this powerful lesson from spearheading a series of extensive polls and focus groups over almost a decade to listen to women about their concerns, hopes, dreams, and priorities for public policy. We found strong similarities across all of the divisions where we expected differences—age, political party, race, generation, even region of the country. Most women shared some critical values and visions that, on balance, diverged from those of most men in the control samples. We will discuss women's values and visions in detail in Chapter 5. They include a preference for collaboration, a longer and wider time horizon, greater appreciation of the importance of relationships, and a focus on preventing crises. Other research about the gender gap (the difference between the views of men and women) has reconfirmed these findings many times.[6]

Numerous studies have tried to quantify what causes these gender-related similarities and differences; theories range from brain biology to social conditioning of girls and boys. As a nurse, I am pretty practical and results-oriented. I can accept that we don't know all the causal factors and still work with what we do know about women and men.

Abilities women bring from our life experience, such as networking—building relationships, collaborations, and partnerships—are powerful ways to trump traditional power. As Insiders and partners rather than competitors, we can change systems and institutions to reflect our views, values, and experience. A winning consensus agenda built on shared values will promote progress on long-neglected issues.

Why This Matters to You

You are a busy person. Why should you care about wedging the door open for women and changing the status quo? Stop for a minute and look around at who is making the big decisions where you work or in your town. Are they doing a good job, or do you find some issues continually ignored? Do you ever think your leaders are pretty unconnected to the world as it looks to you?

Even if you have concerns in these areas, you might be saying, "What difference does it make whether it is men, women, or both determining the business plan for a company, the budget for an organization, or the agenda for the city council?" The answer may surprise you. It matters a lot.

With almost fifty years in the workforce, I am often struck by how many times, and in how many settings, I have heard the same series of issues needing resolution. For example, do you and your friends worry about the level of stress in your lives and how it affects you and your family? Do you want to see work and family continue to be two separate worlds or intertwined parts of the lives of all adults? Are you looking for more respect for your contributions (and maybe those of other women as well), whether at home or at work? Do you feel we are missing the boat on meeting the needs of children and families as important priorities? Are you tired of feeling you have to be twice as good or do twice as much work as your male colleagues to get ahead? Do you want to work for a company (or be the CEO of one) that "walks the walk" on sustainability and the importance of the workforce? If so, you are not alone. Business publications are full of stories about how both male and female employees in the new workforce want to help achieve a greater purpose, to advance their careers while being engaged in the community, and to participate actively in the lives of families and friends.

The decisions of business and political leaders on whether and how these issues are addressed are influenced by many factors, and one of those factors is the life experience of men and women. Our current leaders, who continue to be overwhelmingly male, generally have not spent and are not spending much time or energy to create the kind of world many of us wish to see. Lots of women are working at it, allied with men, especially younger men. But the women are often pressing for change as outside advocates or activists. We are still far from having enough Insiders who share our ideas and are charged with formulating and implementing solutions.

To provide fresh ideas and new approaches, we need a significant group of women who are equals in decision making and who can and will make things happen. When a critical mass of women and men decide together how to move companies, communities, or the country, our ideas will flourish. Women will lead the way. As we become full partners in leadership, we will open up frozen systems, provide access and opportunity, change agendas, and see bottom-line improvements for business, society, families—and women. The 30% Solution is a way to bring about this partnership. It will lead to results that are better for you, your family, and your community.

Moving In from the Outside

The women's movement has concentrated on "Outsider" work: advocating, marching, challenging discrimination, and banging on the door for entry to change the way business is done, one company or one law at a time. This approach has brought us a long, long way toward equality. How dramatically women's lives and rights have changed since the days of the suffragettes who achieved women's right to vote in 1920! But with the hundredth anniversary of this landmark coming up in 2020, we need a new road map that adds an Insider strategy.

One of the best descriptions of the impact of women's change-oriented leadership as we move from Outside to Inside is by Anna Quindlen, best-selling author and Pulitzer Prize–winning columnist, who has laid out the importance of "Inside Outsiders" stepping up as managers and executives. Her thesis is, "By its very nature, women's leadership is about redefinition, while men's leadership has been about maintaining the status quo. . . . It's difficult to see that clearly from inside the endless loop of accepted custom." My experience is consistent with her description of how Insiders come with "deeply ingrained assumptions and the inevitable sense of business as usual," and how Outsiders joining the discussions bring "a fire in the belly that breeds a willingness to step off the treadmill of custom."[7] Women—especially when there are enough of us to press ideas collectively—bring a value-added benefit that follows from our differing experiences, generally outside the power structure, and our passion for workable solutions.

The Leadership We Need

Simply put, diverse leadership that looks like America will be better. Balanced leadership will waste less talent. It will take full advantage of the rapidly increasing pool of talented women who are as accomplished in their fields as their male counterparts, and whose management skill set and techniques match the 21st-century realities of a knowledge-based economy and a diverse global workforce. As recent Outsiders, women will also bring a fresh outlook, a willingness to move beyond stale thinking and adapt tactics to find badly needed answers to old problems as well as new ones. We will cast a more critical eye on policies and practices that have passed their shelf life. So far we seem to have underestimated our strength as Insiders—and so has our country. But we have reached another crossroads in the advancement of women.

Let's face it. We need all the good new leadership talent we can get. Bill George, Harvard professor of management practice and former head of Medtronic, has written extensively about "authentic leadership," which he describes as based on inspiring leaders who can bring people together to get things done. Calling for redefining leadership for the 21st century, George says, "People are too well informed to adhere to a set of rules or to simply follow a leader over a distant hill. They want to be inspired by a greater purpose."[8] Authentic leadership isn't and shouldn't be reserved for an elite few or for one gender; George gives examples of leaders such as Ann Fudge, former CEO of the big public relations firm Young & Rubicam Brands; Marilyn Carlson Nelson, who turned around Carlson's, the family travel firm; and Anne Mulcahy, CEO of Xerox, who took over the company in bad times and made it profitable.

Over the years I have worried about where to find the values-based and future-oriented leaders society needs in these fast-changing times and this interconnected world. I have kept coming back to an important fact hidden in front of me: these leaders are more likely to be women than men. You probably know more women than men who listen first before deciding, move toward teamwork and horizontal management and away from top-down hierarchical structures, and focus on diplomacy first rather than using force and power. These traits are all hallmarks of a different type of leadership, one that fits the times.

An example of how this can work occurred when Congress was in gridlock on what stimulus package would help the country in a deep recession. Despite the dire times, the usual partisan warfare prevailed until two moderate Republican women, Senators Susan Collins and Olympia Snowe, stepped forward to forge a bipartisan consensus. We need more of this kind of leadership, which can end stalemates. Obviously men in Congress have reached many a compromise over the years, but women's leadership style is likelier to achieve solutions with less posturing and wasted time.

More Women at the Table Equals More Progress for All

We will get further by reframing the debate on women's advancement from an argument about rights and justice to one promoting positive results-oriented progress for everyone. "Progress," like "success," can be defined in many different ways. I would define it as including increased attention to giving all children a healthy start and stronger focuses on education, health, and meeting the needs of working families. Many of the women—and men—I have met in a long career see a similar need to define "success" as more than status and wealth. Truly successful companies are not just financially viable in the current quarter; they have good long-term returns for both shareholders and stakeholders.

Marie Wilson, founder of The White House Project, puts it beautifully in her book *Closing the Leadership Gap: Add Women, Change Everything.* She says, "To trust a woman is to trust in a different future awash with ideas and lit by the energy of *all* people. It means more options. It means a fairer equation."[9]

A Vision of the Future

Here's what I see in the crystal ball: With balanced leadership, the United States reinvigorates a commitment to both individual and societal responsibility. It has healthier businesses and happier families, with strong supports for working families. Working couples and single moms can begin to replace stressful juggling with an integrated career and family life (even without a full-time partner at home). At work, women's skills, ideas, approaches, and styles are respected—even sought after—because they add to the bottom line instead of being seen as a problem to be tamed. The workplace, regardless of sector or size, has flexibility and equal pay as customary practices.

We can achieve these goals by turning the following dreams into reality. Let's aim to do it by our hundredth anniversary as full citizens in 2020:

We have reached the tipping point and are moving rapidly toward equal representation of women in political leadership.

"Womenomics"—economics as if women really matter—is widely supported as a mainstream strategy to grow a productive economy and eliminate poverty.

A revitalized social compact places a premium on social and personal responsibility, caring and compassion, families and community.

A recognized accountability framework with benchmarks and measurements exists to continue to open opportunity and avoid sliding backward.

Women at the top are expected, not seen as unusual. Young women grow up expecting to be leaders, just like young men.

To accomplish changes like these, women must lead the way from strength. Having more women leaders matters—a lot. Together, as transformational leaders, we can assure more equality, opportunity, and empowerment for all women and girls, not just white middle-class women. A winning consensus agenda built on shared values will promote progress on long-neglected issues. Along the way, women can do better for ourselves and our families.

Our dreams can come true. Step up to leadership. Bring more women up with you. Together we can achieve the 30% Solution and make life better for you, your family, your community, and society. Shared decision making—with balanced leadership—will change the world.

Part I

WOMEN LEAD THE WAY

1 The 30% Solution

The 30% Solution is a proven and realistic way to bring more women up into leadership, alter cultural stereotypes, and influence agendas, resources, and outcomes. Perhaps you have been one of the "first women"—a great first step—but found out your ideas had less effect than you hoped. We now know the catalyst for a wave of change is having at least one-third women at the table. Learning more will empower you to move from aspiration to action, inform your personal leadership journey, and provide more opportunity for you and other women to be transformational leaders.

If you have not heard about the 30% Solution, you are not alone. The mainstream media have devoted almost no attention to the bigger picture of women's progress. They have instead focused on sound bites, conflicts (real or imagined), and "firsts."

Why do the media so often present factoids about women's progress in quick TV interviews or short newspaper articles, without providing the broader context? One reason is that very few women commentators, editors, or producers play a key role in deciding what is newsworthy. Often, without even thinking about it, we are seeing the world through men's eyes and don't realize a woman's perspective is missing.

In addition, controversy sells papers and programs. Therefore, economic and political coverage of women is heavily skewed toward conflict, not progress. You've surely read stories about younger women vs. older women, Democratic (or liberal) women vs. Republican (or conservative) women, working mothers vs. stay-at-home moms, and, of course, the ever-popular feminists vs. anti- or post-feminists.

"Firsts" are also considered newsworthy. Nancy Pelosi becomes the first woman Speaker of the U.S. House of Representatives. Katie Couric is the first woman in a network evening anchor's chair, and Rachel Maddow takes a similar spot on cable news with her own show. Another woman like Indra Nooyi of PepsiCo or Meg Whitman of eBay becomes CEO of a Fortune 500 company. "Firsts" are certainly better than the alternative, and we've cheered our progress as old barriers have tumbled down.

The broader context of such stories, however, is harder to come by. That context would include, for example, the fact that women make up only 2.4% of the CEOs of Fortune 500 companies,[1] a percentage that has been virtually static over about a decade. We seldom see information to make us wonder why this is so, or how the United States compares with other countries, or whether having more women at the helm might rejuvenate more businesses. Some groups, such as The White House Project and the Women's Media Center, have pushed repeatedly to draw attention to the larger story, but the mainstream media seldom cover their work.

Without this kind of information, we may not realize how much further we have to go. Even if we do, without good data and a strategy like the 30% Solution, women often feel defensive in answering the question "Why single out women?" The work of the women's movement eased much of the earlier overt discrimination, so most of us no longer see ourselves as victims. It can be difficult to articulate why more change is needed, and what kind, to reap benefits for society, not simply to help women or keep the count up.

Background on the 30% Solution

Achieving balanced leadership is actually an old idea. Half a century ago, Eleanor Roosevelt pointed out that better decisions would result if women and men talked through issues together and reached conclusions based on their differing views and concerns. Her words still ring true today: "Too often the great decisions are originated and given form in bodies made up wholly of men or so completely dominated by them that whatever of special value women have to offer is shunted aside without expression."[2]

This view must have sounded radical then, and it is still not the norm. But it expresses the core reason why the 30% Solution is important: women do it differently. The British Prime Minister's Office on Women puts it like this: "Equality. Same. Different." Equality means the same opportunities, but the value added by different perspectives can generate different results. We need to get the best of what both men and women have to offer.

How do we get there? The answer is more women at the top—women who are agents of change and want to see more women join them. Critical mass tips the scales.

In many countries, leaders recognize this, and the power equation in government is beginning to change fairly quickly. Some societies, particularly newer democracies such as South Africa, have started with a basic belief in the importance of shared leadership in terms of race and gender as the very foundation of democracy. In drafting a constitution, South Africa focused on men *and* women, not men *or* women. It looked for enough representation to gain the valuable potential of all people. Other countries have also set benchmarks for women's representation of 30% or more, recognizing that the 30% Solution offers a clear direction and tested strategy to reach greater leadership equilibrium.

The progress of this concept was speeded up by the deliberations of the Fourth UN Conference on the Status of Women, held in Beijing in 1995. Attending the amazing gathering of fifty thousand women and men and 189 governments as a delegate for the United States was a highlight of my life. We came together to create a platform that could guide the full empowerment and advancement of all women and girls around the world. The spotlight was not just on justice or human rights or equality for individual women and girls or even for women as a separate class. Instead, government officials (mostly men) and women's advocates alike talked about bigger ideas such as the value of women's advancement in achieving major societal goals of democratic participation and economic growth.

The energizing and informative discussions of equality were refreshingly different from any I had ever heard in the United States. They moved far beyond the important, but limiting, discussions of how to right past wrongs or protect women because they were victims of discrimination. The theme was the strength women added in modernizing old ways. A big question was, "What would it take for women to assume their rightful place as full actors in society so entire countries as well as families and communities could benefit from women's leadership and innovative ideas?" Building on three years of regional meetings and expert seminars, the conference reached a breakthrough on altering the status quo.

Two intertwined approaches were adopted: mainstreaming women and their contributions in sufficient proportions in all realms of society, including the top levels of decision making, and creating special programs to combat discrimination and overcome historical inequities. Here at home, most of us in the women's movement had worked very hard (and still do) on the second approach, an issue-by-issue effort to move women forward and equalize the scales. Although much more remains to be done on that front, it is adding the first approach, more women making decisions, that has the potential to be truly transformative.

Like the women I meet, you most likely want to make a greater contribution without having to face unproductive and unnecessary hurdles. You see yourself as having skills and ideas to contribute to a society that reflects the best of both genders. This is a future that will benefit men and women alike.

In Beijing, I saw a future like that beginning to take shape. Governments, experts, and advocates from the poorest and richest nations debated whether having more women in decision making could be a key to unlocking the development of more vibrant societies. The answer was yes. Advancing women's participation in determining the shape of the future was a core means of enriching that future. Behind this conclusion was a commonsense proposition: you can't expect anything different if you just keep doing what you have always done.

The conference concluded that for society to progress, something would have to change in the ages-old practice of men making the decisions and women pressing from outside the circles of power for a piece of the action. It was time for women to claim their space. As Insiders with enough strength to be heard, women decision makers could champion new answers to meet rapidly altering situations as well as solve lingering problems.

The delegates recognized that women's roles, education, and economic and political involvement were already improving rapidly. These improvements, however, were not in themselves resetting the power tables. What else was needed?

The conference determined that the presence of 30% women in decision-making bodies is the tipping point to have women's ideas, values, and approaches resonate. This critical mass of women has the clout to permanently change power dynamics. The 30% Solution was viewed as the essential catalyst to reach equilibrium in decision making.

The idea caught fire. A global agreement reaching across all cultures, religions, and political systems now declared the importance of having 30% women decision makers to spur economic and social development.[3] On every continent, these ideas have been put into action.

The 30% Solution Gains Traction around the World (Except at Home)

It may seem counterintuitive for legislatures led by a solid majority of men to create mechanisms to bring more women into office. However, legislators around the world have been able to look beyond zero-sum thinking about men losing when women win office.

Immediately after the Beijing conference, the Inter-Parliamentary Union, an organization of national elected officials like our members of Congress, adopted the one-third marker as the goal for national legislatures. Twenty-three countries now meet or exceed the goal, while 101 have changed their constitutions, laws, and/or political party practices to aim for it.[4] These are not only Western, European, or industrialized countries. The eleven countries with the greatest representation of women at the highest levels of government are Rwanda, Sweden, Cuba, Finland, Argentina, the Netherlands, Denmark, Angola, Costa Rica, Spain, and

Norway. Since the turn of the 21st century, women have been elected president or prime minister in the Philippines, New Zealand, Senegal, Finland, Indonesia, Peru, Mozambique, Germany, Ukraine, Chile, Switzerland, Liberia, South Korea, Jamaica, Argentina, Iceland, Panama, and Latvia.

Different countries have different primary motivations for making these changes. Post-conflict societies like South Africa and Rwanda have written goals for women's participation in parliament into their new constitutions to make a fresh start with new players. In these nations, male leaders were often much more involved than women in fighting wars. Women were often victims and then community builders. After the wars ended, the countries shared the basic belief that optimizing the contributions of women and men would make their societies work best. They also believed that setting hard targets for representation would help achieve this goal by bringing many more women into office.

The U.S. government under President George W. Bush also promoted change by adopting hard targets for women in office—but only outside U.S. borders.[5] The government required the new constitutions of Afghanistan and Iraq to have quotas for women in their national parliaments. Progress for all citizens has been very slow, and long-standing cultural, tribal, and religious norms that diminish women's participation still hold sway. The positive story is how women's voices are now heard at the highest level of government in these conservative societies to begin to counter the pervasive problems women face: Afghanistan is now twenty-eighth in the world in women's legislative representation, Iraq thirty-fifth.

Other countries, such as India, have focused on different reasons for changing their laws. These nations believe greater representation of women will intensify the government focus on many crucial issues and will be of economic benefit. Traditionally, almost all local policy makers in these countries were male. They consistently ignored women's critical priorities at the village level, such as safe water, education, and health care, and this attitude impeded economic progress. Having at least one-third women in these important local-level seats, called Panchayat, has had positive results in bringing about an alternative vision of community development with the introduction of streetlights, clinics, libraries, and public toilets.[6] Negotiations are under way to extend the concept to the state and/or national level.[7]

In stark contrast, the United States has greeted the 30% Solution with silence and inaction. It is barely halfway home to reach the one-third mark for women in Congress. In 1996, the United States was forty-second in the world in women's representation, and it has slid down further and further (see Chapter 3 for details). Other countries are passing the United States up while it complacently moves along at a snail's pace.

In fact, Americans are still debating the role of women in governing the nation. In 2008, polls showed that almost one-third of voters were concerned about whether a woman could be an effective president. In contrast, the first woman prime minister was elected to head the Sri Lanka government almost fifty years ago.[8] Strong and well-known women have also headed other governments, including those of India (Indira Gandhi), the United Kingdom (Margaret Thatcher), Israel (Golda Meir), Ireland (Mary Robinson), the Philippines (Corazon Aquino), and Norway (Gro Harlem Brundtland). The political atmosphere in Norway is exemplified by a story Gro Harlem Brundtland used to tell: her son asked, "Mother, can boys become prime ministers, too?"

Why the 30% Solution Results in Better Government

Women in government are more likely, regardless of party, to concentrate on improving health care and education, on ending violence, and on developing long-neglected supports for working families, such as public policies to promote workplace flexibility and limit the need for family/work trade-offs. They are also likely to fight for better policies for women (with the exception of the "hot button" issue of reproductive health). In addition, women in political leadership tend to bring a different temperament to public policy discussions, with more listening, more collaboration, and less "gotcha" competition.[9]

The experiences and priorities of an all-male governing group may be so different from those of women that certain issues are simply not recognized as important. Top concerns raised by women are often trivialized, filtered out, forgotten, or never moved to the top of the "to do" list.

An example is offered by Senator Mary Landrieu (D-LA), who is also the mother of two young children. At a White House Women's Economic Summit sponsored by my organization, the Center for Policy Alternatives, Senator Landrieu asked, "Do you really think if the U.S. Senate was comprised of 91 women and 9 men we'd still be just talking about good child care instead of making it happen?" (Today, with a record 17 women senators out of 100, the question still stands.)

Senator Barbara Boxer (D-CA) points out that having even a few women in the halls is crucial, but it is often not enough to affect outcomes. Priorities naturally will change more quickly when a critical bloc of Insider women strongly make the case and have the votes. Senator Boxer was a member of the House of Representatives during the Senate confirmation hearings on Supreme Court Justice Clarence Thomas, who had been accused of sexual harassment by a former colleague, Anita Hill, a distinguished law professor. Boxer and six other women members of Congress climbed the steps of the Senate and knocked on the doors of the most powerful senators to plead their case about taking allegations of sexual harassment seriously when judging the character and suitability of someone who would sit on the Supreme Court. Boxer writes, "The seven of us were the only group of women in the country who could get at all close to where the decision over Clarence Thomas would be made. It's hard for me to explain how it felt for seven grown women, experienced in life and politics, to have to pound on a closed door, to have to beg to be heard on a crucial issue that couldn't wait."[10] Clearly we are overdue to have more women as Insiders, not just knocking on the door asking permission to speak on our behalf.

The 30% Solution Improves Business Outcomes

Several years ago Norway, with its history of women leading the country, passed legislation mandating that all publicly held companies have 40% women on their boards of directors or face losing their corporate charters.

(See Chapter 9 for more detail.) The Norwegians looked at growing their economy and improving business performance in a refreshing way—by bringing new leaders to the table. The concept has been very successful, and now other European countries are moving in the same direction.

Catalyst, an independent research organization, has published multiple studies in this country showing that Fortune 500 firms with more women on their boards make considerably more money than those with fewer. The firms ranking in the top 25% in number of women board members generally have higher returns on equity, sales, and working capital than those in the lowest 25%. Moreover, companies with at least three women directors do considerably better on these measures than those with fewer.[11]

Other researchers have found similar correlations between more women decision makers and better returns. McKinsey, the business consulting firm, put its review of the literature this way: "The gender gap isn't just an image problem: our research suggests that it can have real implications for company performance."[12] New studies show that in Europe, particularly in France and Denmark, financial firms with more women at the top fared better during the 2008 economic meltdown. These results are mirrored in the United States.[13]

Some business leaders are making major changes in their companies to gain a competitive advantage by actively reaching for the 30% goal. Deloitte & Touche USA is a large accounting firm that has followed this course since 1995, when it unveiled a women's initiative. Now it reports its success as due in great part to more women in leadership.[14] At a conference on advancing women in the global workplace, Sharon Allen, chair of the board, talked proudly about the firm's multiyear initiative to operate more profitably by closing the leadership gender gap. The results for women are also impressive: at Deloitte, 35% of partners and 30% of directors are women.

Deloitte was proactive in changing its ways to reach this goal. A study of the "brain drain" of talented women leaving the firm showed a lack of role models and mentors, a lack of flexibility, and the presence of assumptions about whether women would be able to handle the best (and toughest) assignments because of family responsibilities without asking them. With a renewed institutional climate of "men and women as colleagues," women must now be considered for every assignment, and retention rates are equal for women and men.[15]

Having one-third women at the top leads to greater opportunities for women at all levels, and businesses stop losing out on half the talent in the country. This is especially critical in good economic times, when there is a war for talent. Catalyst reported significant findings about the internal changes that take place when more women are on corporate boards: "Companies with 30% women directors in 2001 had, on average, 45 percent more women officers in 2006." More is clearly better—having two or more women directors was 28% better than having just one in terms of opening the door for more top women staffers.[16]

Finally, a higher percentage of women in high-level positions makes it more likely that efforts to modernize old customs in favor of employees and their families will be prioritized as societal issues rather than marginalized as "women's issues." And these changes in turn will benefit companies: policies that help integrate work and family life have been shown to decrease absenteeism and turnover.

In the United States, the proportion of women corporate directors is nowhere near 30%, despite the strong correlations between a critical mass of top women and greater profitability, more opportunity for talented women, and an increased likelihood of corporate leadership on family and work policy. The United States is missing an opportunity other countries have grasped. Futurist Mary O'Hara Devereaux tells business leaders, "In 8 of the top 10 [U.S.] companies, women are leading innovation. . . . Firms that are not women-friendly and family-friendly won't get the talent they need."[17] Some of the most competitive countries in the world, including Switzerland, Denmark, Sweden, Finland, and the Netherlands, are also doing the best at closing the gender gap. Germany, eighth on the competitiveness list, is eleventh in closing the gender gap.[18] These countries are taking advantage of their womanpower.

What Can We Do?

How do we push past where we are to where we want to be? More precisely, how can we position ourselves to move society toward goals such as collective decision making, greater integration of work and family, and long-term economic success? How do we get to the place where our leaders take full account of what women have to offer and want to see? Let's first review some popular tactics that *haven't* done the job.

You know that accepting the status quo, waiting patiently for something to break open for you, wishing on the first star at night, or complaining to your friends won't get you very far. Neither will following the advice of the business pundits (male and female) who sound like Henry Higgins from *My Fair Lady* singing, "Why can't a woman be more like a man?" Acting like men to be "acceptable" as leaders means continuing stagnant workplace practices and giving up the difference that difference makes. Why would we want more women to move into big jobs and then do them exactly as they have always been done?

Another approach that won't take us far enough is focusing solely on individual women's achievement, important as that is. We have already seen how this tactic plays out. Women have moved up one by one and been important role models and leaders. Their efforts to make old styles change, however, have been like turning the proverbial battleship. Many have found it difficult to act on their best ideas when they are expected to be "team players," not "rock the boat," and "be one of the guys to get ahead." And some token women fit the "Queen Bee" mold, take an unhelpful attitude of "I made it on my own (thank you very much) without any 'special' opportunities," and don't help other women advance. In short, singular changes, even lots of them, don't mean all the talented, well-educated, innovative women have an even chance with men to make it to the top.

Finally, we won't achieve our goals by relying on the push from the Outside. We must continue this pressure but also increase our number of Insiders who share those goals. I have seen both sides of this need. As a

---

Takeaways

Quick Facts to Speed You on Your Way

- Having one-third women unlocks the door to change.
- 189 countries, including the U.S., have ratified the 30% Solution.
- Women bring new answers. In India, having 30% women officials at the village level changed the agenda to bring the villages clean water, schooling, and prenatal care.
- Companies with more women directors have higher returns on equity, sales, and working capital.

---

longtime women's activist, I have seen lean times when no one Inside both cared about what women want *and* had the authority to move on these issues. And for parts of my career I have been an Insider with various degrees of authority and responsibility, and advocates "banging on the door" were essential to give me the ammunition to press for new ideas.

What *will* get us where we want to be is balanced leadership, a critical mass of women at decision-making tables. And to get that critical mass, women have to make the case, build momentum, and articulate a vision of a better future worth working for. We will have to promote the positive benefits of adding the difference women make and steer away from negativity and finger-pointing. Because of where we have been, it is tempting to fall into victim-speak: "We are discriminated against." Ending discrimination remains an important fight—and we will find it easier to end discriminatory practices with more women at the top.

Claiming discrimination, however, is not likely to be successful as an argument for balanced leadership. A "right to higher positions" contention backs many men into the corner to protect their "rights." And some women, especially younger women, also feel strongly that an argument about discrimination smacks of "us vs. them." Instead, we need to emphasize the benefits of balanced leadership for everyone in our society.

Ahead are some strong historical headwinds and tough oppositional efforts to protect turf. We won't get to the goal in a straight line. Changing cultural attitudes takes work at many levels. Many will say balanced leadership is impossible, unrealistic, pie in the sky, or not worthwhile because "we've always done it this way." Plenty will tell us we don't actually need more women at the top, or say it won't make any difference, or figuratively pat us on the head and tell us to "wait our turn."

Women should feel no acceptable limits. As presidential candidate Hillary Clinton said in her concession speech, referring to the primary votes she had received, "There are 18 million cracks in the hardest of glass ceilings and the light is shining through and the path will be easier next time."[19]

Practical Ways to Move toward the 30% Solution

Stepping into the shoes of the people you need to influence makes your arguments stronger. Let's look, then, at where the self-interest of power players matches recruiting and retaining more women at the top.

In business, CEOs and others in the C-suite (the corporate top brass) are charged with producing a healthy bottom line by increasing profits and shareholder value. Successful companies have the best talent in place to increase their odds of doing this. Reducing the chances for women to make their contributions can only hurt these companies, especially in industries and fields where there is a shortage of talent. Yet only one-third of the top 1,500 corporations have *any* women in top management. In addition, a self-reinforcing, closed management style has led many a company down a dangerous financial path. Shareholders and others seeking change can spotlight the stagnant nature of management composition and the research on how overreliance on "old boys' networks" limits competitiveness.[20]

Companies' desire to be recognized as the "best" creates additional opportunities to gain traction on the 30% Solution. Firms, particularly those with consumer products, compete each year in spirited efforts to be at the top of the "best companies" lists of *Working Mother* or *Forbes*. Looking good is a corporate marketing strategy, so even local awards programs by women's organizations can have great influence when pushing internal changes.

This Week I Will . . .

✔ Look for examples in my own world of the 30% Solution in action—
where enough women are at the table to set a different tone or
direction.

✔ Check out the organizations, associations, and businesses I care about
to see if enough women are at the top to open it up, and begin to talk
about the benefits of the 30% Solution with others.

✔ Understand how the 30% Solution can be applied by reading the
section of the Beijing Platform for Action on women, power, and
decision making.

Pressing for change in politics requires a different set of arguments.
Political leaders are in business to get their candidates elected. This means
we need to identify strong women candidates, set goals and establish programs to facilitate their election, and work to win votes for them. Parties
across the globe have put voluntary programs into place to have more
strong women candidates running to win elections. In cases where these
programs fail, increasingly countries are legislating both benchmarks and
timetables to increase the proportion of women in their elected bodies.
In the United States there is an aversion to such benchmarks. Based on
the reality that women are the majority of voters in every state, however,
political parties have plenty of room to get serious about a wider talent
search to win elections and internal policies to make sure it happens.

Since 2004, the Democratic Party has been fielding twice the proportion of women as candidates for the House of Representatives as the
Republican Party, and they are getting elected at a higher rate as well.[21]
There can be a positive spiral here. In India, for example, women have
been emboldened by seeing the success of other women elected as public
officials. More are running for office and winning.

Competition can help here, too. Right now twenty states have no
women representing them in Congress. According to the Center for American Women and Politics, in the more than 200-year history of our country, four states have *never* had any—Delaware, Iowa, Mississippi, and

Vermont. Women can challenge political leaders of both parties to elect at least one woman to Congress from every state. Larger states could set greater goals, and the challenge could be extended to be sure viable women candidates are running in every election for new senators. New practices could start in any state and spread across the country at every level.

Finally, winning elections in many cases means winning the women's vote, because women are the majority of voters. To get more women to vote for women, we can spread the word that, for all the reasons discussed earlier in this chapter, having more women in power is better for society and benefits all women.

Going Forward with the 30% Solution

It is women who must take the lead in achieving the 30% Solution. Waiting for someone else to do it won't work. Though challenging, the task is not impossible for the tenacious, creative change agents that we have shown ourselves to be. Just as we have beaten the odds to win the equality that has already been achieved, so we can gain the power to make systems more responsive. Together, we can instigate a cultural shift away from long-held biased attitudes conferring "leadership" on men. We can change tired, old-fashioned power structures and systems. And although this will take energy and strength, momentum will continue to build as we get from a few to many women in power.

Our allies will be men who also care about the benefits the 30% Solution brings. Many men have been waiting to be asked to join efforts for women's advancement, and many are seeking a world characterized by the values women are more likely to bring to the table. My husband and son are two of them, and I'm sure you know many others. In speaking about the 30% Solution across the country, I am heartened by the positive response of men. A hunger for new and effective leadership is seemingly stronger than any push-back against my message—sometimes to the amazement of radio talk show hosts who have had me on their shows.

One of my friends recently told me, "No matter what the numbers show, being born as a girl in this country is still far preferable to being born as a girl in most countries in the world." She's mostly right—but not necessarily so for girls born into poor or minority families. A critical mass of women in leadership can help make certain she will be really right in years to come. The 30% Solution can lead the way to a healthier bottom line for companies, for the country, for each of us—and for our daughters, our granddaughters, and the girls of the future. You can help lead the way from a few to many women making the decisions that influence our lives.

How do you begin your journey to step up to leadership and change the world? As a first step, you need to inoculate yourself against a series of social and cultural stereotypes that might hold you back. The next chapter will help you do that.

2 Modern Myths and Stereotypes

Forewarned is forearmed. Understanding the facts on women's current roles and challenges will start you on the journey to being a leader shaping events. You will understand, be able to challenge, and help dispel some self-reinforcing cultural attitudes left over from eons of history during which men have been recognized as the power figures.

Close your eyes and imagine a "leader." What do you see? Extensive studies show that in the United States, the visual image for almost everyone is a man. The higher-level the leader is imagined to be, the more likely this is to be true. Despite the presence of "first women," we are still perceived as Outsiders to leadership—sometimes even by ourselves.

This may seem strange, since women's (and men's) roles have changed in so many other ways. No longer are women assumed to be housewives, waiting at the door in our crisp aprons to welcome home our breadwinner husbands. Likewise, younger generations of men have turned away from the "father knows best" family to a more egalitarian one (though maybe not as quickly as many women hoped). Why, then, do the outdated roles of men as leaders and women as followers have such sticking power?

Who Is a "Leader"?

Communications researchers tell us that we all have "frames" in our minds to help us process big concepts and deal with new information. When new facts don't fit the frame, the default is that the facts are ignored and the frame remains. So far, the frame for "leader" and "leadership" is masculine. This is reinforced in the historical (and sometimes still current) teachings of many religious traditions, including those of Christian, Muslim, and Jewish fundamentalists, that the man is the head of the family and the wife has a more constrained role. Men are the only recognized church leaders and keepers of the faith. With such long-standing mores, no matter how many factual stories appear in the news about individual women as leaders, the frame remains the same.

The masculine frame for leadership seems to depend heavily on perceptions of one quality: decisiveness. During the 2008 presidential primaries, the Pew Research Center conducted a survey on whether men or women make better leaders. A summary in the *Economist* showed how ambivalent we are on who should be in charge; we think women have what's needed but still favor men for the role: "Americans say that they think women are more likely to have the qualities needed to make a good leader. In the end, however, more would still opt for a man in charge." Why?

Of the various qualities of leadership, women were rated far, far ahead of men on being "honest," "intelligent," "compassionate," "outgoing," and "creative," and were considered just as "hardworking" and "ambitious" as men. Men were perceived as excelling only in being "decisive."[1] The preference for men as leaders, then, suggests that the frame for respondents emphasized the role of decisiveness in leadership.

Whenever decisiveness is the primary or only leadership skill identified and men are perceived as more decisive than women, the quick mental picture of a leader will be of a man. Many women were not thrilled when President George W. Bush identified himself as "the decider." The late-night shows made us laugh by saying it made too many of us remember our first husbands. But this bald statement won votes and applause for him as a "strong leader."

Frames can eventually shift, however. If we rate skills where women shine as the essential ingredients in leadership, the leadership frame will begin to shift. For example, if perceptions of women remain the same but creativity and compassion are seen as critical characteristics of leaders, having more women as leaders will become the more obvious choice.

Changing this frame is more than a semantic move. The frame of women as Outsiders rather than leaders is a powerful subconscious influence when current bosses choose candidates for promotion or voters choose their representatives. Partly because of mental frames, making it to the top rungs of anything is still tougher for women than for men. The dominant frames support sexism, the "old boys' network," and discrimination at work. In politics, public-opinion research confirms American voters still think of men as the natural contenders for top positions despite the 2008 campaigns of Governor Sarah Palin and Senator Hillary Clinton. Until the frame of "leader" opens up to include women and the definition of "leadership" includes a broader range of skills than decisiveness, women will be at a disadvantage.

We know decisiveness is not enough to make a successful leader, and you can take steps to mitigate this framing. Practical applications are all around you. When you draft your resume, describe yourself or a colleague for a promotion, write a job description, or suggest someone for an association office, think about a balance of skills—including those at which women excel and, if appropriate, decisiveness. Inadvertently reinforcing the importance of the current definition by making decisiveness the only or most important criterion is a mistake. So, for women, is leaving it out.

Women are also disadvantaged by a frame that places undue emphasis on their appearance. Women running for public office have plenty of stories to tell about how reporters describe their clothes, ankles, cleavage, or hairstyles (often in unflattering terms) before covering what they have to say. Female concert musicians know "blind auditions," where they try out by playing behind a curtain, are much more likely to result in being selected for the orchestra—unless the judges can see their high heels. The same psychological challenge exists for most women to be taken seriously and get beyond the distraction of remarks about how they look or sound as women. The Women's Media Center and Media Matters have produced a video and petition campaign to point out the negative network and cable coverage of women, "Sexism Sells, but We're Not Buying It," which is full of examples like the Fox News headline "Clinton's Nagging Voice Is the Reason She Lost the Male Vote."[2] Numerous articles have also shown the impact of this intended or unintended distortion in academia, business, the courtroom, medicine, science, and the ministry.

The ministry provides a poignant example. Reporting on research from Duke University, the *New York Times* noted that while women make up 51% of divinity school students in mainline Protestant churches, which have been ordaining women for decades, they only hold 3% of large congregations with regular attendance of over 350 people. "The Rev. Dottie Escobedo-Frank, pastor of Crossroads United Methodist Church in Phoenix, said that at every church where she has served people told her they were leaving because she is a woman."[3]

A further complication is that women cannot simply shift the leadership frame by demonstrating decisiveness—or other forms of assertiveness—in the same ways men do. When women speak out, we are often tagged as whiners. When men speak out, they are seen as "take charge" types.

Among ourselves, over dinner, in conferences, or as mentors, women have talked about, complained about, and laughed about how ridiculous this is for years. What feels different and very positive to me is that a few male commentators are pointedly mentioning the unnecessary negative scrutiny faced by women leaders. Nicholas Kristof, columnist for the *New York Times*, has stated: "The broader conundrum is that for women, but not for men, there is a trade-off in qualities associated with top leadership. A woman can be perceived as competent or as likable, but not both."[4] In short, when it comes to manifesting decisiveness, we are "damned if we do and doomed if we don't."

The Double-Bind Dilemma for Women

In fact, "The Double-Bind Dilemma for Women in Leadership: Damned If You Do, Doomed If You Don't" is the title of an exceptional business research study released by Catalyst and sponsored by IBM.[5] The researchers interviewed senior business executives from the United States and Europe to examine stereotypical attitudes that hold women back as "atypical leaders." Their findings make it clear why you and other women still find it daunting to be chosen for and accepted in leadership positions in business—no matter how skilled or talented you are. My experience has been that the double-bind dilemma continues to hold true at upper-management levels in politics as well. Three forms of this dilemma can diminish women's chances to compete equally and be a problem for you.

"*Extreme perceptions*—Women leaders are perceived as 'never just right.' If women business leaders act consistent with gender stereotypes, they are considered too soft. If they go against gender stereotypes, they are considered too tough."[6] Tom Toles, political cartoonist for the *Washington Post*, caught the tone exactly in a nine-panel cartoon during the 2008 elections. Hillary Clinton is at the lectern and a voice from the side describes her: "She's a robot. Calculating. Distant. Cold-blooded. Machine-like. Stony. Emotionless." Then Hillary sighs, and the voice says, "Hysterical female."[7]

"*High competence threshold/lower rewards*—Women leaders face higher standards than men leaders and are rewarded with less. Often they must work doubly hard to achieve the same level of recognition as men leaders for the same level of work and 'prove' they can lead."[8] Women of color face the biggest odds. Indra Nooyi, who is the CEO of PepsiCo and on the Forbes list "100 Most Powerful Women in the World," said when she accepted the CEO position, "Being a woman, being foreign-born, you've got to be smarter than anyone else."[9]

"*Competent but disliked*—When women exhibit traditionally valued leadership behaviors such as assertiveness, they tend to be seen as competent but not personable or well-liked. Yet those who do adopt a more stereotypically feminine style are liked but not seen as having valued leadership skills."[10] Early in my career I hoped to be liked as a boss but decided that it was more important to be respected by my colleagues as being mission-driven, good at my job, and fair. To a large degree, it meant separating my social life from work.

The first person who identified the double-bind dilemma was Kathleen Hall Jamieson, now professor at the Annenberg School for Communications at the University of Pennsylvania, in her book of the same name. She carefully laid out the reality of the conundrum but went on to refute the "women as victims" idea. Instead of feeling discriminated against, Jamieson set out effective marching orders for all of us to move forward by focusing on how women's strengths have brought about an inexorable wave of change. As she said, "They [women] have systematically exposed the fallacious constructs traditionally used against them, and changed and enlarged the frame through which women are viewed."[11] She saw reason for optimism, and there is more today.

Women will overcome no-win double-bind dilemmas by refusing to accept them, expanding the definition of acceptable skill sets, and becoming increasingly capable of meeting challenges successfully. We can keep enlarging the frame of "leader" to include us. The women who follow us should not have to endure these double binds in the first place. Women should not have to play the game to be more like men or face a more arduous climb because of an outdated model of leadership.

Answering Fairy Tales with Facts

To become recognized leaders with our own style, we must also confront and refute some other unhelpful story lines. Worth particular attention are five self-reinforcing "blame the victim" myths that make it seem it is our own fault that women do not have an equal chance to move into leadership. These oft-repeated stories about women and leadership are really just fairy tales. Accurate information can empower you to say, "That's simply not true, and here are the facts."

These five insidious fairy tales are the Patience Myth (Don't be impatient, wait your turn—it's just a matter of time); the Women-Lack-Drive Myth (Women don't want to compete for the top jobs); the Drop-Out Myth (The smart, savvy women are dropping out to stay home); the No-Discrimination Myth (It is only happenstance that everyone at the top here is a man—we're gender neutral); and the No-Qualified-Woman Myth (We can't find women with the skills we need, and anyway, our customers don't want to deal with a woman).

All these myths are pervasive, and to some degree persuasive. Like most urban legends, they contain tiny grains of truth that have been blown out of all proportion. Unfortunately, these convenient stereotypes affect, or even infect, not only current policy makers but our own thinking about ourselves. And they play a big role in stalling the momentum of women moving up in business and politics.

The Patience (or Pipeline) Myth

Many of us have felt comfortable with this idea. Women, maybe even you, have thought, "It's just a matter of time; the pipeline is filling with women, and my chance will come." A lot of advice for women is based on this erroneous idea and usually comes out as, "Just be patient (less pushy) and wait your turn." Many of us who believe our turn will come head back to grad school to improve our credentials so as to be ready for it. Girls are still more likely than boys to fit into this mold, as teachers and educational studies tell us.

You can easily be pretty comfortable when you believe in a wide-open promise of opportunity for your career if you study hard and work hard (or even harder and harder). I hope for your sake this promise comes true, but for many skilled women, for the foreseeable future, it will not. Getting more education is important, but doing it solely because you believe it will bring you promotions is unrealistic. We need to be careful about wearing "everything is fine" blinders.

Wouldn't it be great if having more women in leadership were just a matter of time? The assumption just doesn't hold up very well, though, when you weigh the facts. Chapter 3 looks at how we are doing on taking our place at the power tables where the big decisions are made. The facts there make clear that no matter how you look at it, the pace of progress does not justify complacency. A selection of *New York Times* business section headlines one week in December 2006 made this clear: "How Suite It Isn't: A Dearth of Female Bosses" and "Gender Pay Gap, Once Narrowing, Is Stuck in Place."

The Women-Lack-Drive Myth
(Women Don't Want the Top Jobs)

The Women-Lack-Drive Myth is perhaps more damaging to women's confidence than the Patience Myth. Have you heard statements like, "There really is open competition, but women just don't want to make the sacrifices to fight their way to the top"? Or "If only women were more like men, they'd get more of the big jobs"? Again, there could be a grain of truth here if the assumption of a level playing field were accurate. But it isn't. So we need to ask, are women really more comfortable at less stressful levels? Do we really not want to move up to the top jobs such as CEO?

Careful research by Catalyst on nine hundred corporate executives from Fortune 100 companies shows that men and women equally desire to be CEOs, although circumstances may make attaining the goal impossible.[12] Expectations of top corporate officers, however, often continue to mirror the organization-man corporate life of earlier times. Then, the leader class was almost all men because they had the education, experience, and competitive drive (and women were often kept out by discriminatory policies and a lack of legal protections). The traditional view was work-centric, and the workplace reflected a comfortable view of the world with life and work as two completely separate spheres. It was accepted that work required unending sacrifice to scramble up to the top, and someone at home—generally a wife or paid staff—would manage all the rest of life. This traditional workplace continues to be the model almost everywhere.

The same model dominates in the professions—medicine, law, academia, science. Few women entering the professions have a spouse at home, but most programs are designed as if they did. Dedication and commitment are measured by extraordinarily long hours rather than outcomes. More than thirty years ago Arlie Russell Hochschild wrote, "The classic profile of the academic career is cut to the image of the traditional man with his traditional wife."[13] This could have been written today.

Extensive longitudinal studies by the Families and Work Institute show most women reject the work-centric model in favor of a dual-centric one with family and work intertwined. The traditional workplace, which continues to be the model almost everywhere, is not effective when the pipeline for leadership is filled with women. Women see family and work as "the yin and yang of life," as one focus group respondent termed it. She went on to describe how "take Susie to the dentist for a toothache" and "finish next year's departmental budget" were both on her "to do" list, and she constantly juggles her priorities to manage it all. More and more men are also looking for a dual-centric or integrated life.

Meanwhile, women moving up often feel they face a very difficult reality—stay unmarried or married without children, be lucky enough to have an extremely supportive partner, or find ways to balance work and family in an unforgiving environment. Single mothers have a particularly difficult path to meet their responsibilities and grow to the top of their abilities. Corporations, nonprofits, and governments need good talent—as much as they can get. Women are the biggest pool of underutilized talent in this country. Big changes in workplace practices are in everyone's interest, to make the country as strong as it needs to be. These changes will make families stronger, too.

So, yes, women want to be CEOs—but often not in the traditional mold. And changes to that mold will benefit everyone, not just women.

The Drop-Out Myth (the Smart, Savvy Women Are Dropping Out to Stay Home)

During good economic times, you have no doubt seen stories in the media about how women with top credentials are dropping out to stay home with their children. You might even know someone who decided to take this step. Reality is more complicated, however, and stories headlined "The Mommy Wars" sell publications but don't give the real details.

A few small studies of women graduates of premier universities that were done in the economic boom times of the '90s show that some women who delayed motherhood until they had established their careers chose to spend some time at home with their children. "Chose" is the right word:

most of these women have high-flyer husbands and could afford this choice. First Lady Michelle Obama, an accomplished lawyer, is taking this approach in the White House.

The data are relatively new, and no one knows how widespread the phenomenon is or whether it will hold true at times of high unemployment. It is certain that most women with children have not left the labor force for family reasons. Two-thirds of women with small children are in the workforce, as are three-quarters of those with school-age children. An overwhelming proportion, and a steadily increasing number, of employees living in couples are in dual-earning couples.[14] Most family budgets demand more than one income, so virtually all women in this country will be in the workforce at one time or another while they are carrying family responsibilities for children or elders.

In addition, no one knows whether the women who are "opting out," to use Lisa Belkin's phrase, are making a permanent decision to leave the labor force or work in part-time or consultant positions, or are simply taking a few years to focus on their children rather than their careers. With the stresses of balancing family and work and a desire to give their children the best start possible, many women would choose to follow this route if there were support for the family's income and a way to step back into their careers. Sylvia Ann Hewlett leads the corporate research on establishing "off-ramps and on-ramps" to make this feasible.[15]

For some women, most easily for those with substantial family incomes, the short-term choice might indeed be "stay-at-home mom." A number of families, particularly those doing shift work, are alternating caring for their children as a team. In a few homes, and with increasing frequency, dad is the stay-at-home parent, particularly where the woman is the primary wage earner. In 2003 (the latest year for which data are available), 189,000 children in two-parent households were with dads at home, compared with eleven million children with stay-at-home moms (some of whom own their own small businesses or work part time). Those numbers did not change significantly between 1994 and 2002.[16] Most single moms, of course, don't have a choice at all—they are in the workforce.

This Week I Will . . .

✔ Look around at where the women are—and are not—in top positions at my office and in my community.

✔ Check out my state's record on women in public office and connect up with a group that is making a difference.

✔ Counter any of the myths that I hear with the facts!

It is also true that some corporate women are voting with their feet and leaving hostile environments or family-unfriendly employers to set up and run their own businesses or consulting operations. The top brass in companies should worry about this critical brain drain as their talent moves to more promising opportunities, including woman-owned businesses. What a hue and cry we would hear if all this great talent were moving to another country! Instead, silence reigns. Few large corporations make any substantial changes in response to losing skilled women, and the top layers stay essentially male-only. Taking a blame-the-victim approach, the male leaders claim that "women are dropping out because they want to be at-home moms."

The Drop-Out Myth is also invoked to explain the distressing picture seen across the professions: increasing numbers of women completing graduate school compared with men, but very few making it to the top rungs. Medical literature notes a paucity of women doctors as top faculty; the National Science Foundation reports there are few women in prestigious scientific positions; bar associations cite low numbers of women partners in big law firms; commissions at universities like Johns Hopkins, MIT, and Harvard find a lack of women among tenured faculty or at top academic ranks. Each university or profession seems to think it has a unique problem. However, underlying all of them is an insufficiency of women in leadership. All these reports mention the same missing ingredients: the presence of few, if any, women role models in visible top positions; a lack of respect for women in general, including the differing approaches they bring to the table; and inadequate or nonexistent policies on balancing family and work. None of this has to do with a preference for stay-at-home motherhood.

The Drop-Out Myth is often supported by reference to the Women-Lack-Drive Myth (and therefore shares its weaknesses). But it filters down to a widely held assumption that working moms are fleeing the workplace in favor of home and hearth. It could have a potentially heavy cost to you. What if someone who is doing the hiring assumes that, with a family (or even the possibility of a family someday), you might be here today and gone tomorrow, so it wouldn't be worthwhile to invest in your career? Of course, you would not be told this: after long battles led by women, it is against the law. Unfortunately, if the perception exists in the minds of decision makers and is reinforced in cozy locker-room conversations, it could be just enough to tip the scales to choose a man for the job.

What is really happening is not that mothers are dropping out of the workforce but that men are perceiving them as insufficiently committed to it, based on their view of the customary way of doing business, and penalizing women based on that perception. Ellen Goodman has described this phenomenon in a memorable way: "You can expect to be 'mommified.' Mothers are still treated as if they were a third gender in the workplace. Among people ages 27–33 that have never had children, women's earnings approach 98 percent of men's. Many women will hit the glass ceiling but many more will crash into the maternal wall."[17] Ellen Goodman is right. Young women are closing the wage gap, but only until they have children.

In New York City, these bright twenty-somethings now earn 117% of what young men in the same age bracket earn. No more wage gap for women. But the two reasons quoted in a front-page story in the *New York Times* were these: "In 2005, 53 percent of women in their 20s working in New York were college graduates, compared with only 38 percent of men," and "citified college-women are more likely to be nonmarried and childless, compared with their suburban sisters, so they can and do devote themselves to their careers."[18] Over a lifetime, even with a fast career start, many women will not fit this second criterion—but most will still be in the workforce. Then the "mommification" begins.

Here is the bottom line on a potentially destructive myth: women are *not* blithely deserting the workforce en masse to be at home with their families. The "Mommy Wars," in which at-home and at-work mothers reportedly snipe at each other's choices, are equally fictitious. E. J. Graff, an investigative journalist at Brandeis University's Schuster Institute for Investigative Journalism, has documented the "Mommy Wars" as media hype. She traces years of circular coverage based on shaky data in the "elite triumvirate of the *New York Times*, the *Atlantic* and the *New Yorker*." She says, "The Mommy Wars sell newspapers, magazines, TV shows and radio broadcasts, as mothers everywhere seize on the subject and agonize, in spite of themselves. 'Every other week there's an article saying that if you don't work, you're in trouble financially and if you do work, your child is at risk,' a single mother of three who works part-time told me.'"[19] Saying your child is at risk is a major guilt trip, especially if being at home is not a feasible option.

Though the Drop-Out Myth is just that—a myth—polls do show women across the board see the need for supportive policies so all families can decide what works best for their children without the false "choice" between family and work. Later you will learn more about MomsRising, an online organization that is advocating for a Motherhood Manifesto on important issues for moms (most affect dads, too), whether they are at home or in the workforce.

The No-Discrimination Myth
(It's What You Do, Not What You Say)

As you will see in Chapter 3, we are currently stuck at very low proportions of women at the top rungs of anything—as CEOs, as top corporate officers, as state or federal legislators. What about the ever-popular idea that this is coincidental? Many an annual report claims the organization is diverse and gender neutral, but pictures of leadership circles "just happen" to show all men.

These days having no women at the top and claiming no discrimination is really a mark of poor performance by those in charge. With the pipeline filled with qualified women, when all-male leadership "just happens," you can be sure no one is working very hard to diversify the leadership team. Smart companies have started to invest heavily in diversity strategies because they understand the workforce now doesn't, and in the future won't, be made up of only men (especially white men).

The No-Discrimination Myth is just so much rhetoric. Whatever is in question—a company, an organization, a government entity—if it has totally male leadership at the top, it isn't gender neutral; it is just another exclusive club.

The No-Qualified-Woman Myth
(No Woman Had the Skills We Need)

No doubt in the past, it was often true that employers could not find women with the high-level executive skills they needed. It is true no longer. However, the myth is often repeated, along with its companion, "Our customers/ clients/staff don't want to deal with a woman." Leaders who take this approach have no interest whatsoever in finding qualified women or in seeing their expertise utilized. Their untested assumption is that qualified women aren't out there because their networks (or golf buddies) don't include any. These executives can look across their landscape and feel quite comfortable they are right. The approach is arrogant and shortsighted, however, and self-defeating for their firms.

A colleague recently told me that she and some friends, all alums of a major public university in her home state in the South, noticed that the university had no women on its board of trustees. They contacted the chair of the board and the president, who both said they were quite interested in having women appointed but, unfortunately, had no qualified women candidates. So the women did a lot of research and submitted a hefty portfolio of top women whose accomplishments (and politics) matched or exceeded those of current members of the board.

Three vacancies came and went with no women in the final cut—all the positions were filled by men. The group asked for a second meeting. The president's assistant returned their call and thanked them for their

Takeaways

- Progress to the top for women is slow or even stalled.

- Women are the talent pipeline for the future. Much womanpower is still untapped.

- New ways to work that allow everyone to integrate family and work will break the logjam.

- As you step into leadership, bring more women up with you—we can do better!

work but said there was no reason to pursue this further. Indifference was matched with inaction.

The women are now organizing a network that has as one of its goals having more women appointed to boards and commissions in the state. They have included women elected officials who have some control over the purse strings for this university. Change will come, but it shouldn't be so tough!

As for the tired old myth of customers refusing to deal with women, in a world where women do the bulk of the retail buying (including big-ticket items like cars and health care), this chestnut should be retired. However, in more traditional societies—in my experience, from the United Kingdom to Japan, from Asia to Latin America—it is still repeated. American or multinational firms operating in other countries used to act as if it were true, but change is coming here, too. Particularly in newer industries such as communications and finance, many are finding they are tying their hands on attracting and utilizing the best talent rather than helping the business by bowing to old customs.

Taking the Next Step

Let's bring this down to ground level. Should we just hope the way forward will open up commensurate to the talents and experience women bring to the table? Should we be hampered by "blame the victim" myths such as claims that women are dropping out or opting out, thus "proving" we don't really want to move up? Do we accept the fairy tale of a level playing field or buy that having all men at the top is "coincidence"?

Look around. What does progress look like in your company . . . or your state . . . or on the board of your professional organization or business? Are you comfortable with the current situation? If it doesn't provide room for talented, skilled, and qualified women like you to move into leadership roles in your field, what can we do about it?

Understanding the Patience Myth is false means action is needed. Just waiting in line won't open opportunities in a competitive world. I'm betting on women to lead the changes to make balanced leadership a reality. To help motivate us, the next chapter gives some cold, hard facts on how far we have—and haven't—come.

3 The Everywoman Quiz

Many myths exist about how quickly women are moving up the ladder. With this "Everywoman Quiz on Women's Progress," you can test yourself and your friends on how well women are doing. The facts will help you discard the pervasive "good girl" myths about women's inevitable rise.

The Patience Myth—the pipeline is full of women, so you must be next—does contain a grain of truth. Women are, indeed, swiftly gaining intellectual heft and consumer and voter clout. As a result, the conventional wisdom is that women in the United States are progressing nicely on all fronts. Unfortunately, our strengths are not yet being translated into filling the power positions with the authority to change the status quo.

This quiz will make sure you and your friends have an accurate perception of the progress women are making. The answers follow.

---

1. Over the last twenty years, women have been pouring into college and graduate school. One-third of young women aged twenty-five to twenty-nine have college degrees, compared to one-quarter of young men. Which figure below is closest to the percentage of bachelor's and master's degrees being earned by women today?

   ○ 50% ○ 55%

   ○ 60% ○ 45%

2. Women business owners generate $1.9 trillion in sales each year. That equals the gross domestic product (GDP) of:

   ○ China ○ Brazil

   ○ Russia ○ Mexico

3. The United States has always been a global leader on women's advancement. How does it stack up against the rest of the world? Today the World Economic Forum ranking of 128 countries places the United States . . .

   ○ 16th ○ 27th

   ○ 8th ○ 35th

4. State legislatures are the farm team for women moving into Congress. In 1993, these legislatures included 20% women. Which of these figures is closest to where we are now?

   ○ 35% ○ 25%

   ○ 30% ○ 40%

5. Globally, more than one hundred countries are increasing the proportion of women in public office by legal or voluntary strategies, while the United States is not. Which of these is closest to the U.S. rank in women's congressional representation?

   ○ Top 10 ○ 70th

   ○ 50th ○ 30th

6. This is a consumer-driven economy. What proportion of consumer decisions are made by women?

   ○ 50%   ○ 80%

   ○ 45%   ○ 65%

7. Time is as important as money to career women. Fewer than one-half of full-time workers in the private sector have *paid* sick leave, and only a tiny number have *paid* family or maternity/paternity leave. What are the labor standards around the world?

   ○ Only five countries do not require paid maternity leave

   ○ 145 countries require a week or more of paid sick leave; 98 countries require fourteen or more weeks of paid maternity leave

   ○ One in twelve of *Working Mother*'s 100 Best Companies offers paid maternity leave of twelve weeks or more

   ○ All of the above

8. Based on current rates of progress, how many years will it take for women and men to have an equal number of corporate officers in our largest companies? Hint: Women now hold 14% of Fortune 500 corporate board seats.

   ○ 73 years   ○ 29 years

   ○ 47 years   ○ 10 years

9. The gender wage gap produces different average lifetime earnings for women and men. How much does it cost college-educated women by midcareer?

   ○ $440,000   ○ $150,000

   ○ $250,000   ○ $370,000

10. As a professional woman, have you ever said, "If only I had a wife"? Almost half of men making more than $75,000 per year have a nonworking spouse. What percentage of women at that level have a nonworking spouse?

    ○ 20%   ○ 35%

    ○ 40%   ○ 15%

Answers

1. **Women now earn an average of *58%* of bachelor's and master's degrees.**[1] Women see education as a doorway to success and a decent quality of life and have invested heavily in being well educated. Women under fifty are more likely than men to be college graduates.[2] Among eighteen- to twenty-four-year-olds, 43% of young women attended college, compared with 30% of young men. Now women are surpassing men in attaining associate, bachelor's, and master's degrees and are virtually tied with men in attaining doctorates and professional degrees. (The exceptions are degrees from business schools and in the physical sciences.) The National Center for Education Statistics expects these trends to increase.[3] Because of our great investment in education, women's skills are suited to the knowledge economy.

2. **The sales generated by women-owned businesses equal the GDP of *China*.** Women entrepreneurs are a powerhouse for our economy, with women-owned businesses starting twice as fast as other businesses over the last twenty years—even if they are flying under the radar.[4] The more than ten million women-owned small businesses add up to big business, generating $1.9 trillion in annual revenue in 2007. That was equal to the GDP of China, Italy, or France and only exceeded by the GDPs of Germany, Japan, and the United States.[5]

3. **Would you believe the United States is *27th* in the world in women's advancement?** Unfortunately, it is true. The World Economic Forum, best known for its premier meetings of top executives from around the world in Davos, Switzerland, issues an annual report, "The Global Gender Gap Index." The United States ranks 27th out of 128 countries—behind Barbados, Lithuania, and Mozambique.[6] The series of reports started because these key world leaders—overwhelmingly men—saw women's advancement as a business strategy to increase economic growth.

4. **Women now make up *24%* of state legislators—**up from 20% fifteen years ago.[7] A career ladder of sorts exists for women in politics, leading

from local or state office to national positions. Increasing 4 percentage points at the state level over fifteen years is awfully slow progress. Ten states have now passed the critical 30% threshold (Vermont, New Hampshire, Minnesota, Arizona, Colorado, Maryland, Hawaii, Washington, Oregon, and Maine). New Hampshire is the first state to have a majority of women in its state senate. It offers quite a contrast with South Carolina, which has no women in the senate and only 9% women in the legislature. While women are increasingly moving into powerful positions, the 2006 elections *reduced* the number of women state legislators in twenty states, primarily because of a drop in Republican women legislators.[8]

5. **The U.S. Congress is made up of 83% men and 17% women. This representation of women places the United States *69th* in the world.**[9] According to the Center for American Women and Politics at the Eagleton Institute, Rutgers University, the United States is at an all-time high for women in Congress. However, it is painfully clear that the United States is falling further behind many other countries. The pace is being set by a wide variety of nations, not just a few Scandinavian ones known for their leadership. The United States lags many African countries: as mentioned earlier, Rwanda, with a new constitution, now has more than three times the U.S. proportion of women in its national legislative body. The United States also trails fifteen of its Central and Latin American neighbors, including Argentina, Peru, and Mexico; numerous Asian countries; and, as you probably expected, an overwhelming number of Western nations.

6. **Women make *80%* of consumer decisions in this country,** including on big-ticket items like cars and health care. As *Business Week* says, "Rising female consumer power is changing the way companies design, make and market products—and it's about more than adding pastels." Women's buying power has increased as more women head households, live longer, work more hours, and work their way up the ladder.[10] Finance has been the lead industry in changing how to reach

women. Financial firms have a vested interest in reaching women, who are expected to control 60% of the wealth in the country by 2010. Women are moving up, creating businesses, and earning higher salaries, leading to more wealth. Life expectancy data show another factor: an average age of fifty-five for widowhood.

7. **The answer is** *all of the above* **because minimum labor standards elsewhere have increasingly leveled the playing field.** The United States is really out of the ballpark compared to its international competitors in realizing what changes are needed to assure women and men have a realistic opportunity to use all their talents at home and work. Only five countries have no paid maternity leave (the others are Lesotho, Liberia, Swaziland, and Papua New Guinea). Fully 145 countries require provision of a week or more of paid sick leave, and more than one-quarter of these provide fourteen or more weeks. Ninety-eight countries offer fourteen or more weeks of paid maternity leave. U.S. families have none of these supports.[11] I learned more last year on a visit to Portugal, which provides free maternal care, 120 days of job-protected leave at 80% of salary (which can be taken by the mother or father), and time off for prenatal appointments and breast feeding. It could make American families jealous.[12] In fact, only one in twelve of *Working Mother*'s 100 Best Companies—widely seen as the top tier for family-friendly policies—offers paid maternity leave.

8. **It will take** *73 years* **to reach parity between men and women on corporate boards in our premier Fortune 500 firms.** Momentum has virtually halted, with women's representation hovering at around 14%–16%. In 2006, the number of companies with no women directors increased, and the number with one or two women decreased.[13] As discussed elsewhere in this book, when 30% of directors are women, more women come into top corporate management positions.

9. **Could you use another** *$440,000*? The wage gap really adds up. Mid-career women today are missing out on close to one-half million dollars when you compare the average earnings of college-educated

women and men employed full-time and full-year who were twenty-five to twenty-nine in 1984 and are now in their mid-forties. Dr. Heidi Hartmann says, "Women in their mid-40s today can tell you what their half-a-million lost dollars could have bought: a graduate education for themselves, a top-notch college education for several children, a house, nursing home expenses for an elderly parent, or a retirement portfolio, among other possibilities."[14]

10. Only *20%* of married women employees—virtually all of them professionals or managers—making $75,000 or more have a nonworking spouse, according to a study of over 150,000 employees of major corporations by Corporate Voices for Working Families. Career women are missing one ingredient that has propelled men to the top—a stay-at-home spouse. About half of married male executives in the study have a wife at home. With similar high-earning jobs, women and men are in different places unless we tackle outmoded workplace practices.[15]

Are you surprised by any of these answers? You might have heard some or all of this information in the last few years in newspapers or on TV, but women tell me the "here today, gone tomorrow" stories really don't resonate in their busy lives.

No matter how you look at it, the pace of progress does not justify complacency—or support a recommendation for patience. In fact, we should be *im*patient. Women have tremendous strength and potential—especially in a knowledge economy where education, innovation, and creativity are important skills. But our accomplishments have not been matched by movement into the positions where we can affect the turn of events.

Believing that all is well for women already can sap your confidence if you are not moving up yourself. Our confidence gap is broader than that, though. Too many examples of this gap are around for it to be just another myth. When I talk about it before audiences of women, it resonates all too well. We sometimes make our own boxes, not stepping up to the leadership challenge. We tend to underestimate our strengths or lack confidence in our background or ability to do the job or figure out how to cope. We look next at how you can break out of such a box by understanding and strengthening your Personal Confidence Factor.

4 Breaking Out of the Box

All too many women see their lack of upward mobility as a strictly personal issue. If you feel this way, think again. Accomplished women fail to throw a hat in the ring because of a hesitant feeling of being "not quite ready" for a step up. Personalization of what is really an important societal problem not only holds you back as an individual but contributes to an even bigger problem by reinforcing the old stereotype that women don't want to lead. The confidence factor is not an issue for everyone, so there is a fine line here. If you have an abundance of self-assurance as a leader—congratulations! Skip this chapter and go on to the next. If not, read on.

When I began this book, my focus was helping women move up by addressing the systemic or societal barriers to our advancement. I had two questions: What is holding back the movement of women into leadership positions in government and business? and, How can we more quickly gain the added value of women's strengths?

As the book evolved, my questions led me back to the 30% Solution. It was exciting to see the international progress made since I had first heard about this road map to balanced leadership. I saw more women with influence who could wedge the door open for still more women, shove aside

Could This Be You?

Former secretary-general of the United Nations Kofi Annan, a very wise man and a promoter of women's equality, once told this story when confronted on why there were not more women in top civil service UN jobs.

"I've always been interested in seeing talented colleagues move up, and in my experience, many of them are women. So, whenever an opening for a promotion was advertised, I often said to a talented person, 'You should apply for this job.'

"Women almost universally told me they weren't experienced enough or didn't have sufficient background. I never had a man say anything but 'Thank you, I will apply.'"

systemic barriers, modernize workplaces, and shift long-standing cultural and political attitudes.

I started out to tell this story, but something happened that I hadn't expected. In place after place I heard women questioning whether they should or could move up when opportunities came along. Some were concerned about the consequences of failure or about looking too strong in contrast to their husbands. Others worried about women leaders in their communities who didn't view themselves as being empowered to make the changes they saw were needed. Political women told me how women seldom volunteered themselves as possible candidates, no matter how qualified they were, until asked by someone else to consider running.

Business publications have also noted this diffidence. They describe excellent women's executive leadership programs but say firms often choose the candidates because women don't sign themselves up. And incredibly skilled women starting their own consulting businesses are very nervous about setting prices for their services based on the worth of their expertise rather than the hours they work.

Learning all this, I began to ask a different question: What stands in the way of talented, capable women accepting the leadership challenge when it presents itself? One answer is that self-confidence is in too short supply for too many women. Most women lead in their homes, but too many of us feel we are somehow not quite ready to lead in the larger world of work, politics, and community. We're ambivalent: while realizing the depth of woman-talent and noticing that current leaders aren't really doing such a terrific job, we fail to see how we ourselves can be part of the solution. And if we don't see ourselves as leaders, how can we expect others to do so?

Breaking out of this box is important. System change will come faster when talented women stop "taking it personally" and treat closing the leadership gap as a societal or public problem to be addressed. The place to begin is with each of us realizing our own leadership potential and confidently claiming our place. Women in twelve focus groups from Wall Street to Main Street told me they felt "isolated," with their skills "untapped." They, and other women they knew, had found it very hard to move up, often despite working "twice as hard" and being "better qualified." But abstract conversations about this were quite different from an analysis of what was preventing progress upward. These wonderful women often felt professionally stymied and personally frustrated at not being heard, but—and here's what's important—they often explained it was due to their own inadequate education or training or experience. They believed they needed more of these before they would be "ready." From an objective point of view, these beliefs were often incorrect.

Being a leader means having the confidence to use your personal power to take action and change what needs to change for the better. You won't reach this point—and women won't either—unless we begin to recognize our own potential and strive to be strong leaders wherever we are to make a difference in people's lives.

We are certainly moving one by one into positions of authority and responsibility. A sprinkling of women leaders is seen in virtually every setting. Apparently not all of the women in the focus groups think of themselves as leaders with the potential to create needed change—but they should. With a leader mind-set—and confidence in ourselves—each of us can do more to validate and expand our own leadership capacity, increasing the chances we will be ready when opportunities arise.

Can we empower ourselves to be the leaders we want to see? The answer is yes. Mahatma Gandhi famously said, "Be the change you want to see in the world." Getting there, however, will take some personal introspection and action to increase your Personal Confidence Factor.

Gaining confidence is complicated to some degree by the experiences of your generation and/or profession. As women have prepared to move into wider circles of influence, we have often found locked doors. For example, women financial leaders in a focus group in Chicago—most in their late fifties—shared a sense that talented women they know remain ambivalent about power. They saw women like themselves as just moving beyond a past where women were the victims of power to a future of exercising power in a different way.

Younger women activists in nonprofits in a New York City roundtable discussion saw life differently. They felt fully empowered to be confident leaders. Most of these self-directed young leaders had already created or built organizations to reflect their values and were now beginning to look at campaigning for political office as the next step.

Other women in this "millennial generation," however, had encountered workplace obstacles that had changed their view of what is possible. For some, a women-friendly atmosphere in college had built confidence but had perhaps also encouraged unrealistic expectations. When these young women embarked on entry-level professional jobs in business, seeing their expectations unmet tore down their confidence. Hannah Seligson, twenty-six, writes, "I was born in 1982—about 20 years after the women's rights movement began. Growing up in what many have called a post-feminist culture, I did not really experience institutional gender bias. 'Girl power' was celebrated . . . when I was in college, the female students excelled academically, sometimes running laps around their male counterparts. . . . There was a feeling of camaraderie, a sense of helping each other succeed. Then I left the egalitarianism of the classroom for the cubicle, and everything changed."[1] The corporate workplace simply has not kept up with the changes in the workforce.

How is your confidence? Are you looking for outside validation of your ability? Is that realistic, given the current reality for women in the professional world? Have you passed up the chance to compete for a higher position, saying, "I don't know enough (or have the right education or the years of experience)," or "I'd rather stick where I am until I'm ready"? Promise yourself you've done that for the last time!

Many of the hurdles in your path are simply cultural attitudes that haven't changed around you—or inside you. Check yourself to see how much you have internalized or personalized your situation and perhaps missed the bigger picture. The problem may not be about your ability to do the job.

Let's open the lid on this box and personally empower ourselves to be confident leaders. Remember, upward mobility for you is not just about you. It is also about something bigger—opening the door for more and more women. In Chapter 5 we'll talk in more depth about the "difference 'difference' makes" when a critical mass of women move up. That cycle can't start unless you and others step up.

A Check-up for Your Personal Confidence Factor

As you look back at your own life, maybe you can see times when you said "No, thanks, not now." Perhaps you were asked to be an officer of a club or president of the PTA or your synagogue or church guild and said, "I don't know enough." You might have passed up an opportunity to take on a challenging assignment or position or go into partnership with someone or run for the school board. Was your reaction based more on a reflex than on careful assessment of why someone thought you could do the job, or whether you might actually have been able to do it well? Maybe you assumed someone else would be better qualified than you without even looking at the other potential candidates.

To check your Personal Confidence Factor, take a look at the following questions. They are based on common situations that could sap your confidence if you are personalizing the problem of career mobility. Each question can give you ideas on how to move forward.

Have you ever wondered if something is wrong with you because you haven't been promoted or appointed, made partner, or gotten tenure? Have you noticed whether other women are in the same boat? Do you feel you have to be twice as good as male colleagues to move up, and resent it—but not seek promotion because you are sure you won't get it? Or do you assume the work world is like college and you don't have high enough marks? Myra Hart, a retired senior faculty member at Harvard Business School who studies women as entrepreneurs, explains, "By and large women believe that the workplace is a meritocracy, and it isn't."[2]

Do you feel overwhelmed in shouldering your responsibilities as a parent and a professional with little or no support from your boss or the community? Are you stressed out and frustrated, even angry, when your effort to be the best you can be—as an employee or boss, as a mom or daughter, as a volunteer who gives back—is not respected and is even diminished as "trying to have it all"? Have you felt accepting a new challenge would automatically mean a high cost in family stress and personal guilt, without balancing all the factors carefully or thinking about how you could change them a bit from a new perch?

Did you compete successfully for a better job and then fail to negotiate for salary, working conditions, flexible scheduling, or other benefits? Strong data show that women, in contrast with men, seldom negotiate when presented with a job offer or a pay raise, then often feel personally left out or passed over when they discover inequities among their colleagues.[3] If you didn't get the job, did you assess why and identify what you needed to do to compete better? Did you think hard about whether it is time to move on to greener pastures or stay where you are and increase your ability to tackle the higher-level job—or did you internalize the setback as a personal failure?

Have you told yourself you were unprepared when what you really felt was uncertain? Were you worried about failure or suffering from an unrealistic internalized expectation that you should be able to perform really well from Day One without a learning curve? An expectation of performing perfectly is a real barrier for many women, especially when you see no one who looks like you who has ever done the job before. Did you worry about failure having negative ramifications for other women rather than looking at how success could have positive ones?

Did you take yourself out of contention to move up into a pretty solidly male domain because you figured you'd have to become "one of the boys"? Did you worry about feeling out of place in a command-and-control environment when your style is more collaborative? Did you consider whether you might learn a lot from some of these men as peers, mentors, or partners, or whether helping other women and like-minded men move up with you could change the internal culture?

Have you fallen into the "perfectionist trap"? Are you the first person in the office in the morning, the last to leave, one of the few who pass up vacations and take a full load of work home on the weekends? Is this really what the job requires, or are you requiring it of yourself? Are you possibly being taken for granted? Have you made yourself the "go to" person, then felt put-upon but told yourself you are too valuable to the mission where you are to move out or up?

Are you excessively risk-averse or afraid to fail? Are the standards against which you measure yourself realistic? Are you getting negative energy from family, friends, or coworkers that tears you down rather than building you up? Do you feel like you are walking on a tightrope? Are you? Have you looked to see if there is a safety net? Have you developed a support network, or have you been "too busy"?

Are you concerned you might be a token woman with little voice or power to change what needs to be changed? Are you afraid that your great ideas would just be credited to someone else, or that women would expect too much of you? Are there ways you can claim ownership of your contributions? Could you be a role model or a mentor? Lone women can begin to make changes, although it takes more talented and qualified women with you to gain momentum.

If some of these questions fit you, the answers probably affected whether you stepped up to meet a leadership opportunity. When you overdo the questioning of your own ability, compare yourself unfavorably with others, have a martyr complex, or see only problems ahead rather than opportunities, the likelihood is that you become overly cautious and stay put.

Changing the world starts very close to home. Weigh your first instincts and look far enough ahead to see how moving up in leadership could give you the opportunity to do something differently. With power often come the right and responsibility to take charge and begin to change the customary ways of doing things. Without someone like you in authority to challenge the status quo, changes can't be expected—and we will never get to the tipping point.

Getting Over It: Personal Thoughts on Negotiating a Difficult Terrain

I'm not sure exactly why lack of confidence was and is such a common issue for women, including me. Clearly socialization is part of it. In my generation we had few female role models and were expected to defer to male authority figures—fathers, bosses, teachers, husbands—and not to make waves. Winning approval and being "good girls" were often synonymous with not confronting authority and doing whatever needed to be done without question (including getting everyone coffee).

This model was hardly designed to improve the confidence of girls or women, and it had powerful effects on many of us. For example, despite an excellent high-school academic record, I turned down a four-year all-expenses-paid college scholarship in nursing, instead entering a hospital training program. I didn't think I could do college-level work, and no one advised me differently.

Perhaps, at least to some degree, I bought—and some of us still buy—the image of ourselves as the "weaker sex." It is a vicious circle. Lack of confidence makes us feel (and act) less decisive; perceived lack of decisiveness means we are not viewed as leaders; and when no one else thinks we can be leaders, it is hard to get or stay confident.

Here is a way you can buck yourself up that works for me: turn the *unthinkable* into the *impossible* into the *inevitable*. The remarkable woman who taught me this decided to interview and then convene all of the living female presidents and prime ministers from around the world. Imagine how implausible this must have seemed when Laura Liswood, now the secretary-general of the Council of Women World Leaders, first thought of the idea.[4] Under Laura's leadership, this council has brought together the top elected women in the world since 1997 to improve governance by increasing the number, effectiveness, and visibility of women leaders. A ministerial initiative regularly brings together all women who are cabinet ministers in various areas, such as health, environment, and women, to share ideas and strategies.

We often both underestimate our individual strengths and gain little oomph from the collective strength of women standing behind us. It seems as if we have not internalized our own importance and potential. Women's educational levels are soaring, and our consumer, investor, and political clout are following suit. Although we are still having difficulty getting enough of us into leadership, heads-up organizations are starting to see they must fully utilize womanpower. When they do, the payoff is stellar results. Thinking about yourself as an integral part of this high-potential womanpower will lift you, too.

Build Your Own Confidence, and Others Will Have More Confidence in You

Empowering yourself isn't easy for many women, but it is time to move on. Good strategies, courses, networks, and resources exist to help you. Many other women have faced the questions of how to step up and then to cope with mastering a new environment. Stories of women like you who have gotten up their courage, swallowed their fears, and done what needed to be done will energize you. Entrepreneurial women have set a great example. They epitomize this idea: failure isn't a problem, but failing to pick yourself up and learn from it is. Here are some other women's ideas to help you take a leap of faith, overcome personal doubts, and step right up to being a leader others will view with appreciation and respect. The more you work on taking these steps, the more you'll increase your Personal Confidence Factor. And it's a positive spiral: the more you increase your Personal Confidence Factor, the easier you'll find the steps.

Step One: Be Ready When Opportunity Knocks

Be open to serendipity. Possibilities pop up when you least expect them and can change your life in pretty astounding ways. You will often have the clear option to accept and walk through the door or decline. Saying yes may mean not standing on ceremony or being willing to turn your carefully scheduled life upside down. My introduction to women's international work, which paved the way to an ambassadorship, came when I was invited at the *very* last minute to join the delegation to a UN meeting in New York in 1994.

On a more romantic note, my husband of thirty-five years and I met when, on two days' notice, my boss asked me to go to Mexico for a meeting as a replacement for someone who was ill. I was a single mom, and saying yes looked impossible. My friends came to the rescue. Off I went on my first international business trip—and met Keith, a delegate from the United Kingdom. As they say, the rest is history.

Try to welcome even the opportunities you would not have chosen. Supervisors who believed more in my ability than I did myself gave me some really tough assignments. At times they even had to push me to try. The really good ones answered my questions, picked me up if I fell, and celebrated with me when I succeeded—all of which raised my confidence for the next time. You might be able to immediately put this technique into action and build not only your own confidence but that of people working for you.

Step Two: Stand Up, Speak Out, and Make a Difference

Following your passion will help build your confidence and leadership skills. You will find it easier to stand up, speak out, and make a difference on the issues that most concern you, those that are close to home but have a wider impact, so they don't feel self-serving. Think for a minute. What is your "top of the mind" problem, one you know needs to be solved, and on which you can make a difference? The variety is endless—a new traffic light for young schoolkids, neighborhood problems, recycling at work, environmental issues, a stewardship project at church, registering voters. Whatever the problem is, your help is needed. You might even consider joining the board of a group working to address it.

The benefits of getting involved are twofold. Your passion will help your cause, and your efforts will build your skills and increase your self-confidence. Experience with "selling" a cause can improve your ability to "sell" your skills and talents. Many very talented women have told me this is a tough personal assignment for them even though they realize it is important to compete for leadership positions or clients.

Consciously reflect on how the skills you practice in fighting for something you care passionately about can be transferred to presenting yourself well in professional arenas. In my case, responsibility for lobbying and fund-raising forced me to gain confidence. Both bring with them far more "no" than "yes" responses, but you can't get to "yes" without a positive, confident approach (even if you are shaking in your boots). To get back up and put myself forward was often difficult, but it got easier the more I did it. Without question it was part of my job, so I put some flowers on my desk and a smile on my face and stepped up. Over time I began to like both, and to my great surprise, I found out I was good at both. I remember having one of those lightbulb moments when I realized that presenting my nonprofit's projects to foundation program officers took the same set of skills I had used to advocate for better educational policies for the members of a large teachers' union. This realization was a turning point for me in becoming a successful fund-raiser. Until then, fund-raising had felt like begging, and I had hated it.

Women around the country have told me that what is important to them is an opportunity to "make a difference" and to "give back." What surprised me is how few understood the way volunteering can directly translate into improved confidence to articulate what you believe in, make a sound case, and work with others to reach a shared solution and execute change. Sharpening these skills starts with the first time you speak in your own authentic voice at a hearing, run a silent auction for your favorite charity, write a letter to the editor, or advocate for a candidate or issue. Practice is important.

You may also have to practice increasing your visibility. Extensive polling finds that "what women want" starts with being taken seriously and respected for our contributions. This is a pretty low bar, but as long as only a few women are at power tables, you are likely to have the following experience: As one of the few women in a meeting, you make a suggestion. The chairman simply moves on to someone else (a man) at

---

Takeaways

- Don't be boxed in by a lack of confidence.

- Check your Personal Confidence Factor.

- Turn the *unthinkable* into the *impossible* into the *inevitable*!

- Be ready when opportunity knocks.

- Stand up, speak out, and make a difference.

- Seek linkages so nothing you ever do is wasted.

- Practice confidence-building skills: negotiation, finance, communication.

- Decrease the odds of failure.

---

the table. The discussion continues, and ten minutes later one of your colleagues (a man) makes the same suggestion you did. The chairman and others at the table congratulate him for the great idea. What can you do?

You have several options. Some are not very useful: saying (politely or not) "Hey, that was my idea"; joining in the jolly congratulations without making a plan to do better the next time; seething with frustration and reporting the slight to your girlfriends. Alternatively, you could use the incident as impetus for finding ways to strengthen your voice. Some possibilities are finding male and/or female allies for your point of view before the next meeting, drafting an options paper on the problem to be discussed at that meeting, or offering to develop an implementation plan. All of these improve your odds of being part of the solution as a member of the team. Being purposeful and strategic strengthens your voice more effectively than complaining. And the more you do it, the better you get.

Step Three: Look for Linkages and Connections

In writing this book I have had a fellowship from Demos, an excellent and growing network of ideas and action in New York. Miles Rapoport, its president, has this sign on his desk: "Nothing you ever do is wasted." It is true.

If you want to enter (or reenter, or move up within) politics, business, or community organizations, for example, think about how many related skills you are already using in your everyday life. Scheduling a busy household is similar to arranging for coverage of a hospital department or an office with flexible working hours. Managing a household budget is a beginning step toward managing a departmental budget. Being a nurse seems like a long way from being a diplomat, but nursing is where I learned to listen well to other people, read body language, and work incredibly hard for long hours. Making connections like this demystifies what skills you already have and what you need to move up as a leader. Here are three sets of skills you might not have thought about that are very powerful and great confidence builders: negotiating, following the money, and communicating.

Negotiating—for yourself, your department, or the solution to a problem—will strengthen your hand. The ability to reach a satisfactory agreement while preserving your principles, continuing to move forward, and protecting your bottom line is at the core of crafting business contracts, legislation, and solutions to critical issues. Negotiating well means not only coming away with a satisfactory solution but preserving face for the person across the table, which will be important in future negotiations. Do you step back from negotiating for yourself or others on changes that you see are needed?

It still does happen sometimes that women who take the lead in negotiation are seen as "pushy," men as "smart." Often, women are afraid of this push-back and hesitate to confidently take the lead. Don't take it personally. I see much more space than is currently being used to negotiate for a better working environment for you and your coworkers.

Following the money is an excellent technique for understanding what is happening in business and government. Follow your own money, too, and you will tackle another common confidence gap. Prudential Financial's studies on women and money describe this lack of confidence as "the chasm that lies between knowing something and doing something about it."[5] Financial columnist Michelle Singletary has noted, "Even though women have moved ahead financially, a number of studies and polls indicate we still have more to achieve and sometimes we impede our progress by our own doubts."[6] Even women making more than $100,000 a year often lie awake at night worrying about becoming "bag ladies" rather than taking charge to manage their money effectively.

Are doubts about money affecting your life? What action are you taking to gain confidence in financial matters? Gaining confidence in your understanding of both personal and professional finance is critical to making good decisions on everything from hiring another worker to planning your retirement. Learning to manage all kinds of resources—revenue, expenditures, people, budgets—is not only central to successful leadership but raises your level of self-confidence in taking risks.

Practice your communication skills so you can write clearly as well as present your views orally in church or synagogue, community organization, union, professional group, or business meetings. Since people place such a premium on decisiveness when weighing leadership ability, how you say things is important. Try to avoid the passive or "feminine" voice, as it is often equated with tentativeness and weakness. A negative introduction to your ideas or outright apology for raising them lessens their importance and impact. If you want to be taken seriously, avoid constructions such as "I'm not sure this is relevant, but. . ." Being direct and forthright does not mean being rude. Listening well and being diplomatic can soften the edges.

I first realized how constraining it was to use circumlocutions rather than direct statements when I was a young nurse. At that time nurses were never permitted to use straight declarative sentences to explain a patient's condition. This would have overstepped our bounds and made us appear to be making decisions, which only doctors could do. I was actually taught to say "I think the patient is no longer breathing" rather than "The patient is not breathing." In health care or any other field of professional endeavor, being clear, honest, and direct is associated with decisiveness and strength, while lapsing into feelings-talk is not.

Step Four: Decrease the Odds of Failure, and Learn from It When It Happens

Failures, mistakes, and setbacks (a bad boss, nasty office politics, outright discrimination or harassment, a lost promotion) all happen to both men and women, but they seem more likely to shake women's self-confidence. "Keeping on keeping on" and repairing your own self-confidence is an ongoing process during the rough-and-tumble of a career. I have found that support from my networks, a much-needed cheering squad, often made the difference, helping me take risks and learn from them rather than fear failure.

You will stumble or fall sometimes. Not many people move up the leadership ladder without unexpected, and even undeserved, crises. Companies fold, merge, and reorganize; the economy falters; good bosses come and go; elections are lost; natural disasters hit; and major health or family problems intrude on carefully laid plans. Our own mistakes also get in the way of a glide path: we hire the wrong person, miss a downside risk, bet on the wrong product or partner, burn out, or run too far ahead of the resources available.

Whatever the problem, will you be able to pick yourself up and learn from the experience? Even better, before a crisis strikes, can you find people you trust and respect to give you feedback, constructive criticism, and just plain help? You will be in a better position if you are proactive, network, and improve your skills and experience as your future safety net.

If you need to pick yourself up after a tumble, volunteer for committee work to learn more and meet new people in your field. Also increase your building-block skills: Get whatever training, mentoring, or remedial education you need. Target the right experience to get you where you want to go. Read and think more broadly and keep learning. See how trends, politics, and current events will affect your company or town. Becoming more of a generalist rather than a specialist will serve you in good stead. All our experiences have unexpected interconnections that open doors to opportunity and change. To become leaders, we have to take the chance to keep learning and growing—without knowing where it will end.

Taking What You Know to the Next Level

When participants in the focus groups and those I interviewed assessed the current situation for women, they saw systemic changes that will help build personal confidence and validate women's management skills and style.

Many are included in the rest of the book, such as the story of Women Leading Kentucky, a mentoring and supportive network for career women in Lexington, Kentucky, and the way Madeleine Albright, then heading the U.S. Mission to the United Nations, brought together the handful of women in similar positions and made important inroads for women and girls in war-torn areas of the world.

The women I talked with are right. It is a time to feel confident and break out of the box. The bottom-line results are positive when more women are change agents or transformational leaders to make a difference in people's lives. The next chapter helps you leave behind past models of leadership and visualize the leaders we need for the future. Women fit this empowering picture.

5 Today's Transformational Leader

Looking at the pace of change around us, it is clear that traditional definitions of "leader" are too limited for the future. A positive shift is taking place toward the skills and approaches women like you bring to the table. Brawn and toughness are out: creativity and innovation are in. There is a need for transformational leaders ready to meet contemporary realities. Recognizing this need will create more opportunity for women to move up and will lead to decisions reflecting our values, vision, and experience.

This century has already brought vast changes, and they aren't likely to slow down anytime soon. The future is obscured. Communities, companies, countries, even the planet, are facing major problems for which old answers don't work. Many feel society is at a momentous crossroads.

A fragile economy built on consumer demand fed by rich credit has been collapsing, with millions of jobs lost and huge financial institutions and corporations disappearing daily. The industrial economy is shredded, with major sectors like the automotive industry finding few customers, and big-name Wall Street financial firms forced to close, line up for federal handouts, or restructure due to a poor business model. Industries like steel are being hollowed out as other countries compete with lower prices. Outsourcing work to cheaper labor markets has been considered smart business. The biggest corporate giants are no longer creating jobs at home; many of them are in deep trouble and have laid off employees by the thousands. Unemployment is rocketing (particularly for men in manufacturing and construction). And despite working longer hours (among the longest in the world), families have seen their incomes stagnate or drop and benefits like health care and pensions become personal responsibilities rather than being shared with employers.

The nature of the U.S. workforce is changing. The country is racially and ethnically diverse, and becoming more so. An aging population and immigration are also altering the picture of the workforce. Men are a bare majority of the workforce, and the Labor Department projects that only 15% of new entrants to it will be white men. Women are a critical source of more people power. And competing in an interconnected global, entrepreneurial, service, and information society requires an innovative, educated, skilled workforce.

Finally, the United States has been fighting a two-front war in Iraq and Afghanistan, draining its national resources even as its manufacturing and financial sectors, infrastructure, education, and health care have fallen behind the times. Terrorism is another long-term threat, with economic and social development to end poverty increasingly seen to be as important as military might (and even military might now includes womanpower). National defense leaders state that as the country's traditional military and economic strength is stretched to the breaking point, its security rests increasingly on diplomacy, energy independence, and women's empowerment.

All these changes combine into a daunting picture. The old rules no longer apply, and it is foolhardy to believe the leaders who got us where we are today will have all the solutions. This country is overdue for a conversation on what leaders are needed for the future. The old leadership profile, which might have sufficed in a stable world, simply won't do now. Instead, the country requires real change agents who can make companies more competitive, the workforce more productive, and communities more compassionate. While the 2008 presidential campaign presented clear alternatives on the path forward, a fruitful leadership discussion must be framed with a wider lens to include more than national politics.

A Time for New Leadership

National polls reflect a deep feeling that U.S. business and political leaders over the last decade should have been better and done more to foresee and forestall problems. Instead, these leaders trumpeted a set of values that are now out of sync with any semblance of stability and security for families, enterprises, and the country. We need transformational leaders, and I know where to get lots of them.

Experts have been dissecting what caused the 2008 economic crisis—the deepest in years—but we already know for sure what didn't cause it: women. One *Washington Post* article was headlined "In Banking Crisis, Guys Get the Blame: More Women Needed in Top Jobs, Critics Say." The article, which was about Europe's approach to breaking up a counterproductive closed culture at the top ranks of business, stated, "Fred, Tom, Andy, Dennis, Eric, John, Stephen, Antonio and Paul ran British banks that lost billions of dollars. So they have been called in for a grilling [by the Parliament's Treasury Select Committee] and in line with the usual math of the financial world, 18 of the key 19 people were men."[1] This is not just finger-pointing; it speaks to the need for a different way to lead.

Balanced leadership with women holding more of the purse strings has begun to be discussed in the United States as well. Nicholas Kristof puts it this way: "Banks around the world desperately want bailouts of billions of dollars, but they also have a need they're unaware of: women, women, women." He adds, "Wall Street is one of the most male-dominated bastions in the business world: senior staff meetings resemble a urologist's waiting room. Aside from issues of fairness, there's evidence that the result is second-rate decision-making."[2] President Obama is among those noting the need for more women in power. In signing an executive order creating a White House Council on Women and Girls, which includes the heads of all federal agencies and is led by Valerie Jarrett, a top advisor and longtime friend and colleague, Obama highlighted the absence of women at the top levels of government and business. He said, "I think we need to take a hard look at where we're falling short, and who we're leaving out, and what that means for the prosperity and vitality of our nation."[3]

Regardless of political party, profession, or position, women are the largely untapped source of the fresh ideas we need. Women like you are poised for leadership at all levels, and we can make a powerful difference as we move up and bring more women with us.

Women Bring Shared Values to Leading

We are used to hearing about the diversity of women's views (for example, the divergent voting patterns of single women and married women). What we seldom talk about is the concerns and vision women *share* and how these differ from those shared by men and therefore from "conventional wisdom," which generally reflects the views of current thought leaders (guess who).

I am convinced from both research and personal experience that women share a potent value set that cuts across the usual fault lines in our society. In 1993, I led a women's economic summit with about sixty top women leaders who were at the top of their game in government, politics, universities, business, and labor and grassroots groups. They came from every walk of life, race, ethnicity, political party, part of the country, and discipline. Expecting that such strong and diverse women would need a long discussion to reach consensus on shared values, we set aside three hours for it. One-half hour later we had full agreement on a list of values the country's leaders should have.

See how your list matches this one from the women's summit:

- A premium on prevention and investment for the future rather than crisis management for immediate problems

- Long-range thinking that takes into account possible unintended consequences for society or the planet, rather than quick or "shoot from the hip" answers

- A life integrating work, community, and family and friends as a goal for everyone

- Value for stakeholders, including stockholders, employees, customers, and society, trumping shareholder value alone as the mark of worth

- Open access to resources needed for success, with emphasis on building relationships rather than closed networks

- Horizontal organizational structures to encourage innovation, not just vertical ones

- A commitment to diversity, inclusion, and equality, with inequality being unacceptable

- Consensus building, not "gotcha" politics

- Sustainable self-sufficiency replacing charity

- Collaboration and partnerships as the hallmarks of successful leadership

Contrast these values with the ones underlying the decisions that led the world economy to the brink. You can probably list some of those values: a premium on short-term profits for shareholders, top-down hierarchical management, rampant competition for bigger and bigger bonuses and CEO salaries, consumption today on credit regardless of tomorrow, crisis management, and acceptance of inequality as "just the way it is." Which set of values do you believe are critical for those exercising power, whether in a small business, a community organization, or the economy?

A solid women-led consensus policy agenda for the country also exists and is actually supported by a majority of men in nationwide polls but seldom reaches a vote. Our solutions are still seen as outside the mainstream, discussed more in women's conversations and publications than in the media or academic circles. For example, for decades women's organizations have advocated for increased attention to curbing violence against women and girls. Because many in power trivialize such priorities by labeling them as special-interest "women's issues," forward movement is fitful despite support by both men and women. Shaking up the status quo is much tougher when you can be easily marginalized.

Nevertheless, acting on our priorities and ideas in the parallel universe of women, we have created positive change through approaches that deserve wider exposure. Women-owned businesses are good at generating jobs even though undercapitalized. Women's foundations are creatively partnering with community organizations to help women-headed families break out of poverty and become self-sufficient. Women's groups like Women Thrive Worldwide along with development organizations like CARE and the World Bank are putting women at the center of turning around poor countries. Effective advocacy partnerships of unlikely allies are working to improve public policy and corporate practice on balancing family and work. The new "moms movement" is campaigning for policies for moms at home and in the workplace. Creative thinking and research by nurses is increasing the possibility of improving health outcomes and cutting costs. Women's networks are providing connections, education, and support to up-and-coming women leaders.

Real change demands transformational leaders who hold the "new" values and agenda priorities rather than the conventional ones. Obviously some women will not agree with these values and priorities, and some men will. But we are more likely to see them reflected when more women are at the table. Change is in the air.

Definitions of "Leadership" Are Moving in Our Direction

I've been interested for a very long time in how women's strengths as leaders guide groups to new answers. My personal experience includes running a nonprofit and a consulting firm as well as working in the macho male environment of the trade union movement and the virtually all-female field of nursing—with every combination of male and female leadership in between.

When I started in my career, one leadership model prevailed everywhere. "Loyalty" ("the boss is always right") was demanded, almost militaristic top-down structures were the norm, "dog eat dog" competition was fostered within and between organizations, and "power" was being able to tell people, "Do it!" and have it done without question. I didn't think much about whether this model brought out the best in me or anyone else. It was essentially the only one around.

In the early '90s, powerful thinkers about women in business and politics started to be heard. Sally Helgesen made the management case for more women in the corporate boardroom with *The Female Advantage:*

Women's Ways of Leadership,[4] and Dorothy W. Cantor and Toni Bernay did the same for women in top political jobs in *Women in Power: The Secrets of Leadership*.[5]

Methods and techniques women brought to the table—collaboration, communication, and consensus—began to gain legitimacy and be seen as valuable rather than a sign of weakness. We began to see a few token women move up every type of career ladder. Gender-neutral concepts such as mission-driven and values-based management with clear benchmarks and metrics for impact and outcomes began to replace the idea of an all-powerful boss who knew all the answers.

By 2007 the business pages were telling a new story about what counts in corporate leadership. The top business columnist for the *New York Times* declared that the "age of the authoritarian CEO is over" and went on to describe the mix of soft skills modern CEOs must have. "[They should be] good listeners, consensus builders, ambassadors to the larger world, and leaders who others follow not because they have to but because they want to . . . informality is important. Charisma is important. Empathy is impor-tant."[6] Joe Nocera was describing a man, but the definition fits women leaders to a T when we have confidence in our personal styles.

What a sea change in the attributes and characteristics of the best CEO material! It sounds a lot more like you, doesn't it? In addition, hav-ing a magic formula for "leadership" isn't accepted anymore. The concept used to be, "Either you've got it or you don't," but now we are on a path where the captain of the football team won't be seen as more of a "born leader" than the captain of the women's soccer team.

Don't get too comfortable, though. A strange thing is happening. More professional schools are teaching the "softer skills" to all students, but women still are not being recruited or promoted to achieve balanced leadership—because we are more likely to epitomize these styles and ap-proaches. Despite the increasing recognition in management literature of the value of a new type of leadership, the old style has remained preva-lent in the everyday world of power figures in business and government. The answer isn't more men learning these skills as much as it is balanced leadership to gain the needed mix.

The Leaders of Tomorrow

Over the years, I've worked on leadership development and tried to flesh out a prototype of the leaders the world needs. I am looking for leaders who are future-oriented and understand how to build from the bottom up on this interconnected planet. I want smart leaders who have high emotional intelligence and can bring people together to meet a mission or reach shared goals. Leaders are needed who listen well—and not just to a coterie of admirers—and build consensus rather than believe they alone know best.

The leaders of the future need to think over the horizon, work collaboratively, and achieve results that are good for everyone, not just a few. They must be problem solvers who work to strengthen the economy without sacrificing families and communities. The nation deserves leaders who commit themselves to empower people to be self-sufficient, and who engage citizens to solve common problems before they reach dramatic proportions. These leaders will believe in diversity and inclusion as strengths. They will work toward a better future including peace, justice, and human rights for all.

Many of the people currently holding leadership positions don't meet my definition and, instead, bring a set of assumptions that reinforce old practices and stereotypes. Women like you can be the leaders who bring strong values, fresh air, and inventive thinking to change outcomes. What skill set will these leaders need? Every text on the subject identifies the same basics, although today's leaders don't necessarily display them. Leaders should be talented, open-minded decision makers who try to have all of the facts on the table, who can get things done, and who are intelligent, competent, and honest. They should exhibit character, wisdom, integrity, and courage. Important—and hard to come by—as these characteristics are, however, they are no longer enough.

The newest management literature adds another list of characteristics required to lead wisely for a better tomorrow. These include imagination, inspiration, and ingenuity. More people skills are essential in multigenerational and diverse workplaces with a preference for teamwork. Leaders need to understand that getting the best from employees takes mutual understanding, the building of relationships and respect, and persuasion rather than force. Women leaders used to be tagged as "indecisive" because we tried to gather as much information from as many sources as possible before deciding and moved toward finding common ground. Now we are right on target with what transformational leadership requires. Last, new leaders must be flexible and used to multitasking, not a bad description for any woman who has raised young children.

In short, the skill set for transformational leadership is a good match with what most women comfortably bring to the table. This newest management literature on what works gives women a further boost as the leaders for the future. Each of us should take it to heart.

Diversity, Inclusion, and Consensus Are Essential

In my experience, diversity around the table is essential to exploring issues fully and making good decisions, no matter the purpose or process. Looking at the world as if the experience of elites (particularly if these are narrowly defined as white middle- or upper-class men) covers the territory leads to narrow decisions, arrogance, and short-term gains at the expense of larger values and goals. Building a common agenda requires thinking about the whole range of stakeholders.

Diversity, in a thriving democracy or a successful business, is about inclusion of a wide range of voices, points of view, life experiences, and ways of looking at the world. It begins with racial, ethnic, and gender diversity. At various times and for some initiatives, it needs to include geographical and socioeconomic balance (particularly to include people who are affected), generational differences, and differences in sexual orientation, physical and developmental ability, and/or political persuasion.

We have a deep reservoir, as yet barely tapped, of wonderfully talented women of every race and ethnic group. Regardless of ability and experience, women of color have faced greatly diminished possibilities to move up even when racial, ethnic, or gender diversity is considered. We will have the new leaders we need when more women of every race and ethnic group have real opportunities to take their seats at the table.

One often forgotten element of diversity is the inclusion of men in efforts to empower women. My husband still remembers the early days of the women's movement, when our living room was a frequent meeting place. Whenever he entered a roomful of women activists, everything stopped dead. He is certainly not the only male supporter of women's equality who has been left outside closed doors. It is urgent that women and men work together for the next stage of advancement—bringing women to the decision-making table as full partners—because both will benefit.

Inclusiveness is not a matter of political correctness. Rather, it builds buy-in and stronger outcomes. Of course, it makes "my way or the highway" leadership extremely difficult. Instead, it demands a different approach, one that is often a hallmark of women's leadership: creation of consensus.

At a focus group in Chicago, a woman state senator stated that creating consensus is an effective leadership tool that she and her female colleagues use to get things done—especially when lots of divergent interests are at stake. Many women elected to office excel at building coalitions and consensus because they began as activists and needed these skills to succeed. As legislative leaders, they use them to bring about win-win solutions on politically tough issues where divergent interests and priorities are at stake. At the Chicago focus group, for example, women leaders cited the use of consensus to create a new Department of Juvenile Justice and a regional planning board.[7]

Consensus is a common way to reach agreement in other countries and in the United Nations. Here it is often misunderstood as falling down to the lowest common denominator. As a diplomat I learned this is a false premise. Consensus building is a process of finding common ground on difficult issues to forge a solution all parties can live with—even if they didn't get everything they wanted. It is quite different from a "50% plus one" legislative approach, which can make the losers extremely put-out, especially if they were left out of the process.

Finding a common starting point or definition of the problem to be solved is the first step to reaching consensus. This can be a challenge in itself. At the Beijing conference on women's advancement, the countries represented had dramatically different histories, views, and track records on women's equality. First Lady Hillary Clinton stirred the participants with her words, "Women's rights are human rights, and human rights are women's rights." Her words created a vision for a common starting point anchored firmly in the Universal Declaration of Human Rights, which recognizes the inherent dignity, equality, and inalienable rights of all members of the human family.

Even with human rights for women as the shared vision, consensus was not reached easily on a blueprint for advancing women's equality. Dealing with issues of women in decision making (which called for the 30% Solution) paled in comparison with the controversies around questions of sexuality, health care, comparable worth, and land and inheritance rights.

The consensus document that emerged, the Beijing Platform for Action, is far from a lowest common denominator. It is a striking, even radical, global road map for women's empowerment. The platform is a living document, and countries in all regions of the world have implemented major sections of it—sometimes willingly and sometimes with the monitoring and advocacy of women's organizations. In the years after Beijing, as ambassador to the UN Commission on the Status of Women, I was surprised to hear country after country—including those with the poorest ratings for women's equality—report new progress against the goals. It almost sounded like a competition on who could move further or faster, no matter what the starting point. The consensus process had worked wonders.

The United States is increasingly diverse and operates in an interconnected world. Our leaders are not in a position to simply impose their will through economic or military action. It is imperative to be conscious and conscientious about the inclusion of all stakeholders—often people with views quite different from their own—and to build consensus. Women's leadership styles emphasizing listening, collaboration, and thinking for the long term can help bring about consensus where now we see stalemate, progress where we see only dead ends.

The Concrete Dividends of
Investing in Women's Advancement

Leadership that looks like America pays big societal dividends. Here is a quick summary; other chapters provide you with research and resources to learn more. Balanced leadership will bring about the following advantages:

Less wasted talent. The talent pipeline is increasingly made up of women. Having women as primary economic actors, role models, and decision makers improves the recruitment, retention, and promotion of qualified women. Women leaders have deeper and broader networks for finding and bringing on board more women. Women executives often lead the way on creating cost-effective practices to utilize the products and services of women-owned enterprises. More women leaders can bring greater recognition to addressing problems women face, such as balancing family and work, and can improve morale, both of which can improve productivity.

A modern management skill set matching the 21st-century workforce. A concentration on partnerships, relationships, collaboration, and teamwork also improves productivity, leading to a healthier bottom line. A wider horizon and more holistic thinking can alter planning for contingencies. A deep understanding of the overwhelmingly female base of retail consumers rewards organizations with a clearer view of "what women want." Effectiveness and efficiency are increased by the use of newer management techniques taking a mission-driven approach based on clearly understood outcomes and deliverables and flat or horizontal organizational structures.

Healthier businesses and happier families. These result from increased attention to policies to integrate work and family life (including flexibility, employee assistance, and assistance with child care and elder care). Proven to decrease absenteeism and turnover, these policies are good for company success and profits as well as employees. Family-friendly businesses make the United States more competitive and align its family supports with those of competitors in the rest of the world.

A reenergized social compact valuing both individual and collective responsibility. This compact is based on the importance of compassion in

---

Takeaways

- Women have a future-oriented set of shared values and fresh ideas to meet changing times.

- The profile of leadership has moved beyond brawn and strength to creativity and innovation.

- Women fit the talent profile for the new leaders we need.

- The concrete dividends are less wasted talent, modern management skills, family-friendly policies, and a social compact based on mutual responsibility.

---

society, of caregiving for families, of giving back to the community, and of investing in sustainable companies that exhibit social responsibility as well as financial viability. Women are 60% of the investors in such companies. Also, polling over many years has shown women, much more than men, believe government should play an active role as a responsible partner with individuals and families for the well-being of those in need, including children and the elderly.

Other countries are investing directly in women as a smart bet for economic growth. Underinvestment in women has been shown to perpetuate poverty and limit economic development. Nobel Prize–winning Harvard economist Amartya Sen has led the way for increased global understanding that "gender inequality is a central concern to social and economic analysis because of its effect not only on girls and women, but also on boys and men. Expanding women's freedoms will contribute to the well-being of all."[8] Steadily increasing attention is being paid to freeing up the full potential of women to improve democracies and economies. The United States lags behind on investing in such women-centered economic self-sufficiency strategies.

Microfinance investment—small loans, generally to very poor women, to start or grow minibusinesses with the support of peer groups—has proved successful. Women have a top-notch record in paying back the loans. For example, the Self-Employed Women's Association (SEWA)

This Week I Will . . .

✔ Write down my list of values, see how closely they match what I see in my company or organization, and check them against women's shared values.

✔ Imagine how my management style might be different if I were running the place. How would having a more family-friendly workplace be better for me? for my organization? for everyone?

✔ Look for a leader who exemplifies the characteristics I think are important. What makes him or her different? How successful is this leader?

---

founded by Ela Bhatt has 350,000 depositors in its bank in Gujarat State in India. The repayment rate is 97% for microfinance loans ranging from $100 to $1,000 with a 15% interest rate.[9] Clearly Wall Street could take a few lessons.

International efforts like microfinance increase women's earnings, lower poverty rates, and secure better outcomes for children. Women are much more likely than men to use new income to meet direct family needs. In Brazil, the probability of a child's survival increases by 20% when earnings are in the hands of the mother instead of the father, according to the World Bank.[10]

An Object Lesson: Having Only a Few Women in Office Costs Everyone

Having more women in leadership brings important dividends and gains for everyone. Conversely, everyone pays a heavy price when there are not enough women in leadership.

My family, for example, lives in incredibly conservative South Carolina, which has the lowest percentage of women legislators of any state (9%) and no women statewide officials. South Carolina also tops the unemployment charts and has a high rate of domestic violence, pervasive poverty, an extremely high proportion of people who are obese with chronic health problems (including heart disease and diabetes), and a scandalous number of children without health care. In addition, it scrapes the bottom on educational levels for women. The price tag for gender inequality in the economy is very high. Research by the University of South Carolina Moore School of Business showed that in 2006 the wage gap (particularly for women of color) and the fact that so many women are undereducated and hold low-paying jobs cost the state $12.7 billion in tax revenues, a figure dwarfing the $7.0 billion state budget.[11]

Whoever Sits at the Table Makes the Decisions

As discussed in earlier chapters, opening up opportunities for women, resolving issues of great concern to us, and creating new ways to do business won't happen without balanced leadership. Someone or something is always going to get the nod, but women can't just expect it to come in our direction if we are basically absent from the important conversations. We have to be there, and in sufficient number to make the needle move. Getting there won't be easy—but power sharing never is. More women as mainstream Insiders will lead the way to a world that reflects our values, vision, and experience.

I believe in the strength of the phenomenal women I have met in every corner of this country to be the transformational leaders we need. You can be one of them. You can start wherever you are and make a difference every day. The next six chapters give you a road map for success.

Part II
STEPPING UP TO LEADERSHIP

6 Starting Right Here, Right Now

We change gears here from building the case for more women in leadership to providing you with some practical tools for stepping up to leadership. You can start wherever you are to make a difference every day and play your part in getting all of us to the place where women's ideas can shift priorities. The Power of One can start chain reactions. Virtually every setting offers you the potential to apply a gender lens, change the status quo, or improve outcomes—and simultaneously grow your personal leadership potential.

This chapter and the ones that follow set out a road map. Our immediate destination is the 30% Solution. It is within our reach, and once we get there, we will be able to catalyze a wave of change to take us further. We'll start by discussing sensible and realistic things every woman could do today and then move on to what you might do if you are the only woman at a power table, or one of just a few.

How can you empower yourself to make change happen as a transformative leader? It starts with thinking differently about what you—as one already busy woman—can do. Decide now to make a difference every day. It doesn't have to take a lot of time or special skills. You can start to change the dynamics at work; in your church, mosque, or synagogue; in a community organization; with younger women and girls; or anywhere you choose. Some of the best leaders I have met are nurses' aides who led hospital organizing efforts for better working conditions. Wherever you begin, the skills you gain—and the people you work with—can contribute to solving larger and larger problems at work, in the community, or in the world.

Creating change requires planning, teamwork, and organizing, but all the best strategies won't get you anywhere without action. Change requires doing. The wise mother of a friend, a woman who had worked all her life as a domestic and raised a large family, used to say, "To start a journey you must take the first step." Taking the first step toward what you want to see is imperative to avoid paralysis or second-guessing that keeps you from doing anything at all. So start today, seizing opportunities as they come along. Midcourse corrections are usually possible if you are careful not to burn your bridges along the way.

Invest Wisely

We each have two resources at our disposal: time and money. Maybe one or both are in short supply in your life at the moment. Don't let that stop you from thinking about how to leverage your resources to advance your goals and move toward the 30% Solution.

Considerable research shows that women are more hesitant than men to make major contributions to game changers like philanthropy or politics. While women have moved forward to support women's foundations, organizations, and candidates, we have a long way to go before we are significant investors in the advancement of women. Women are also reluctant to make this advancement a priority when families make decisions on contributions. This holds true regardless of whether or not we are earning a major share of the family income or are the ones paying the bills.

Look at your own contributions of time or money. Each of us has skills or resources another woman or girl could use to move forward. Here are three possible avenues; the Resources section provides more detailed information.

Do you invest in women and girls in your own community? Do you support organizations that build girls' esteem, like Girl Scouts or school groups? How about community programs to prevent teen pregnancy, end domestic abuse, or elect women to office who agree with your point of view? Have you found a way to recycle your work outfits by giving them to a group helping women be ready for job interviews and work? Have you found your nearest women's fund or foundation?

Do you advocate for policy change? Advocacy is an important tool that is available to all of us to make needed policy changes to smooth the path and make the upward journey easier. Even with very limited time you can educate yourself and act. Make your voice heard on policies to advance women and girls. Future chapters introduce you to some of the effective advocacy organizations, and you can start by connecting up online.

Do you always register and vote? No matter how busy you are, voting is essential if we are going to change what is to what should be. Women's Voices, Women Vote has shown that unmarried women make up one of the largest potential voting blocs, but many are still not registered. A number of states now allow you to register and vote on the same day. Thirty states have early voting, which lets you vote on your own schedule. Vote Smart is a completely nonpartisan one-stop shop for information on how to register, on candidates for national and state offices, and on state referenda.

The Power of One

Inherent power for change exists even if you are the only woman at the table. The Power of One is the way to use your personal influence as an Insider in an office, an organization, a church, or a local political party. Envision a better future for where you are—a future as if women matter. Then reach out and connect up. Build support, empower others to take the incremental steps that can add up to major ones, and celebrate wins, no matter how small. As Women for Women International puts it, "One woman can change anything. Many women can change everything."

How can you use your Power of One to create new opportunities for other talented women and girls through the decisions you make, the people you hire or mentor, and the networks you build? Think about what you bring to the table based on your own experience. What can you do to change an unfriendly atmosphere to a more accepting one and get the job done better? Think about leading in ways that do not reinforce old power structures and styles. Even symbolic choices can mean a lot. For example, young women leaders from the nonprofit world in New York applauded the picture of Nancy Pelosi accepting the gavel as the first woman Speaker of the House of Representatives surrounded by children rather than "old white guys in suits." In contrast, as one woman commented, "[As women leaders] we often still look embattled. That won't cut it." These activists saw a need for the new leaders of the sector like themselves to expand their horizons by making a difference in larger institutions, public office, or business—on their terms.[1]

Even if you are already in a leadership role and accepted for your technical expertise, you can bump up against problems when you try to add the specific value of a woman's perspective. For example, a dean at a state university (one of a very, very few female deans) said her ideas were well accepted until she had a baby and realized the pressing need for child care for faculty, staff, and students. Her colleagues listened but said it was not a priority. As she said, "When I raised an important concern of women, I was patted on the head."

Be confident that you can make a difference over time, although it may be harder and take longer than you would like. This is true especially on a topic like a space for women to pump breast milk, which may seem trivial to the men around the table. Instead of feeling defensive, use your one woman's voice to make clear how a decision will affect women—and how the right decision will improve outcomes. Confidently bring your experience as a woman to the table as strength. Practice makes it easier. If you work to open the door wide, you won't be the only woman for long.

WellPoint, the nation's largest health insurer, now has a "first woman" CEO who offers a great example of how a woman's perspective can help other women and the bottom line. Angela Braly has publicly described her leadership strengths as based on her perspective as a working mother with three children. Her personal experience, she says, is what connects her to the needs of WellPoint's members. Women make 70% of health care decisions, her employees are 80% women, her managers are 60% women, and her board, under her leadership, now has one-third women.[2]

A First Day as a First Woman

I was the first woman appointed to a top position in the New York State Department of Labor. I was also young and a trade unionist, not a winning combination to the traditionally male and crusty upper ranks of the civil service. Seven men with thirty-nine or more years of seniority apiece reported to me. I soon found, however, that my personal life experience was what added value to make my contribution different from those of the men who had held the job in the past.

One of the first issues brought to my desk was described by the personnel director as the need to fire a clerk in the department. Firing anyone in the civil service, particularly in a unionized state, is rare except for malfeasance. The charge here was consistent tardiness: this woman was chronically ten to fifteen minutes late. She was evaluated highly as a very skilled employee and was willing to work late or through her lunch hour to make up the time. But the personnel director believed it was crucial to "let her go as an example for others." I'm sure you can guess the story. As a single mom, she had to drop off her two children at separate locations, and one school did not open early enough for her to get to work on time. As a mother with two children who also had to go in two different directions each morning, I understood her situation.

More importantly, as a manager I could lead the way, not only retaining a good employee but creating better policies overall for our largely female workforce. A flextime policy for the department started right then. Most of the managers fought it hard, and it was launched as a pilot project with one interested manager. When the data from the pilot showed decreased absenteeism and increased morale, we were able to implement flextime and job sharing throughout the agency. We'll come back to flexibility in Chapter 8 because it is still an issue for most people in the workforce.

When You Are One of a Handful of Women

When Madeleine Albright was named ambassador and U.S. permanent representative to the United Nations, only six countries (about 3%) had women in these prestigious positions as the leaders of their country's delegations. Ambassador Albright made a dramatic move on her first day. Rather than holding her first official luncheon with the leaders of other nations on the Security Council, she invited all the women permanent representatives to lunch. They came from various corners of the world and started then to meet monthly, providing each other with both intelligence and support.

These women ambassadors added something to the usual role of representing their countries by bringing a unique set of perspectives to the job. While the media commonly show images of soldiers, guns, explosions, and burning buildings in war-torn countries, these women also saw the forgotten victims of these wars. The UN puts it this way: "The victims in today's armed conflicts are more likely to be civilians than soldiers. Some 70% of the casualties in recent conflicts have been non-combatants—most of them women and children. Women's bodies have become part of the battleground for those who use terror as a tactic of war—they are raped, abducted, humiliated and made to undergo forced pregnancy, sexual abuse and slavery."[3]

The women permanent representatives saw a need and took action. This tiny group of Insiders became a powerful voice of conscience. Working together with strong women Outsiders advocating for women's human rights, they succeeded in getting gender-based violence to be seen as one of the gravest violations of international law. The Security Council had not previously envisioned a role for women in peace and reconstruction. It has now institutionalized having more women in peacekeeping missions to deal with the crimes against women and girls in armed conflict.

If you are a "first woman," or one of only a few, do you know of other women in similar positions in different departments, or on other committees, or who are clients, customers, or other members of your profession? How about reaching out to have lunch? Have you held back because the men in your shop might talk? An excess of caution may keep you from being as effective as you can be or building the networks you need for your career. We'll discuss networking further in Chapter 10.

Preparing Yourself: My Personal Lessons

Looking back over almost fifty years of a career as a change agent gives me some insights into what worked for me. A recommendation from my mother was the single best piece of career advice I ever had:

When the door opens, go through.

My mother believed someone who suggests an opportunity for you probably sees something in you—talent, courage, expertise, or personality—that you had not recognized in yourself. I've heard women say, "Oh, I was just doing my job" and ignore leading questions like "Why don't you run for office? Will you try out for this job opening? serve as chair of this committee?"

My mother was absolutely right about going through doors of opportunity when they open unexpectedly—even if the moves seem counterintuitive. I remember the day when, out of the blue, I took a call at my desk in Albany about a White House position as deputy assistant for women's concerns for President Jimmy Carter. I was asked to come to the White House the next day and discuss the job. Of course I went. I had no expectation of an offer, but I was asked to stay for a second day of interviews. I had only brought a briefcase, so my mother and I went shopping for everything from a toothbrush to a suit. My husband was incredibly supportive, although my taking the position would turn our lives and his career upside down. The door opened, and with great anxiety I accepted a position that dramatically changed my life.

Have you ever ignored the open door or even shut it tight without a look? Many doors get closed unnecessarily. I've expanded my mother's advice this way: "If the door opens, go through it after weighing the worst thing that could happen." What is the worst-case scenario if you take the chance? Will you regret it later if you don't? Check with your support network, then go for it. Often the downside risk is actually pretty minimal or manageable. Being risk-aware is smart; being risk-averse is not.

On occasion you will be the one opening the door for other women. When you do, pass along this advice (which I did in needlework and hung on my office wall):

Life is more than work.

Is it possible to move up and reach out without risking the family balance we treasure or compromising our health? With a 24/7 work world full of BlackBerrys, e-mail, voice mail, and text messages, it is even harder to shed the office for a few hours for family or personal time. Like most working moms, I often felt pulled between the needs of our family and the requirements of the workplace. Guilt was a frequent companion. Finding the positive energy to keep on keeping on was a basic challenge for me, especially when I was a single working mother.

Feeling successful in your life often rests on being able to follow your passion. My choice was to find work that met my passions and brought me personal satisfaction day to day. Even so, as a sometimes overachiever, perfectionist, or workaholic (choose your favorite term), I often tried to be a superwoman on all fronts at once. It was too easy to forget the question I often heard as a student nurse: "If you don't take care of yourself, who do you think will do it?" When I was recuperating from colon cancer surgery I finally understood the lesson that life is more than work, and it has served me well since. Feeling successful also means keeping your energy up for the long haul. While it is hard to pull away, an hour spent perfecting a report beyond perfection won't be as energizing as a walk in the sunshine with your partner or children.

Every job has some potentially draining aspects. Fighting a resistant bureaucracy, constant fund-raising, backbiting, Queen Bees, personnel challenges, tight budgets—they all go with the territory. Learning from your mistakes, continually moving forward, being optimistic and upbeat to lead others effectively and not become cynical—all of this, while necessary, can be both difficult and tiring. Long hours, tough travel, illness (yours or a loved one's), commuting—all can take their toll.

Along the way I've picked up some coping skills to keep up my positive energy quotient. The first and foremost is not to work beyond my strength. Fighting fatigue and stress to keep at it—no matter what—simply doesn't work for me. My relationships suffer and it wears down my energy, immune system, and health. When people say, "I don't know how you do it," it usually means I am overextended—again—and need to rethink priorities, share the work, or shed some of it.

What else helps to keep up positive energy? Here's my list: avoid people who give off negative energy; celebrate successful small steps, holidays, and anniversaries; share fun and laughter with children (your kids and grandkids, nieces and nephews, or the children of friends); build a team of mutually supportive colleagues; follow my European husband's adamant belief in vacations taken regularly as a restorative measure; walk outdoors; do yoga. The McKinsey Leadership Project notes that one vital characteristic of "centered leadership" is managing your energy level. "Identify the conditions and situations that replenish your energy and those that sap it . . . give yourself time during the day to focus without distractions." Two other characteristics of this type of leadership are framing situations positively and finding meaning in your work.[4]

It's easy to fall into the trap of feeling that if you did just a little bit more, the results would be worth the trouble. The problem is, you can't always tell in advance when this will prove true. On some of the issues I care about most passionately, solutions have barely moved despite years of effort, or have fallen apart just when it seemed we would finally make progress. Many an election night, whether in politics or in organizing, has found me bemoaning the results rather than cheering. All this has taught me one more vital lesson:

Take the long view.

A few years ago, a poll was taken at a meeting of top women from multinational corporations in Prague. These women were high flyers making big money, but their strongest personal goal was to be able to retire at forty-five. Why? They figured that at the pace they were going, forty-five would be when they were completely burned out. We need a better way. Otherwise we'll never get to the 30% Solution, and we'll lose a lot of our best talent to sheer exhaustion.

Most American women today who are college educated and watch their health will live to be at least eighty years old. Sequencing life—not simply rushing through it—offers lots of ways to have both family and a meaningful career as a leader in the community and/or the workforce over a lifetime. Melding career and family over a lifetime should be possible for both women and men.

Sylvia Hewlett's excellent research with top corporations shows how more "on-ramps and off-ramps" could allow us to take time off without losing career momentum.[5] The time could be used for raising a young family, caring for parents, sabbaticals, further education, a trip around the world—whatever. As a leader you will find opportunities to open up a longer horizon through flexible working patterns.

Each step I took in this direction as a leader of a nonprofit convinced me that stretching out the work and not overburdening our terrific staff enhanced both morale and productivity. We worked incredibly hard but also knew we—and our friends and family—could stand the pace. The flexibility strategies included sabbaticals, interest-free loans for computers, regular opportunities to work at home, paid parental leave, compressed hours in the summer to allow longer weekends, and shutdowns (except for a skeleton staff) between Christmas and New Year's. These very cost-effective measures were the secret to recruiting and retaining extremely talented staff, even at the unfortunately lower salaries of the nonprofit world.

In looking at these three life lessons—"If the door opens, go through," "Life is more than work," and "Take the long view"—think about yourself first. Numerous studies show women are seldom willing to do this. Framing issues as "good for our daughters" is the conventional wisdom on how to raise these concerns with women. It's time for a big step: self-awareness and care for you are critical to authentic leadership. It really isn't possible to make a difference every day, to think and act as a leader,

---

This Week I Will . . .

✔ Check the job descriptions for higher positions where I can help change current practices in my company or community—and apply.

✔ Inventory what gives me positive energy and try to get more of it.

✔ Use the Web to find a women's fund or girls' organization where I might contribute my time or money to help others step up to leadership.

✔ Start a list of the amazing women I see in my own life from whom I can learn leadership skills—and call one of them.

✔ Share advice from my life's journey with a younger woman.

---

if you are worn out and worn down. You are probably the only person who can change the equation, and you owe yourself the time to do it!

Paths toward a Dream

I could fill a book with stories of the amazing and dynamic women I have met who have made opening doors their life's work and legacy. To help give you energy and ideas, here are thumbnail sketches of four of them: Sara Horowitz, Zeyba Rahman, Connie Evans, and Noeleen Heyzer. They have all taken alternative paths to use their unique perspective as women to create change that works for everyone. Meeting them will give you ideas of new possibilities close to home—in even the toughest environments.

Filling a Niche for Part-Time and Contract Workers

Sara Horowitz, CEO of the 60,000-member Freelancers Union in New York, is a social entrepreneur who saw "a 'disconnect' between working people and the establishment" and decided new solutions were needed. With her background—a labor union family, a Quaker education, professional degrees as a lawyer and from the Kennedy School at Harvard, and experience on a hospital organizing campaign—Sara understood both power and market-based solutions.

Sara told me that independent workers (the self-employed, contract employees, part-timers without benefits, etc.) are 30% of the national workforce. They work hard but fall through the cracks when it comes to benefits. The Freelancers Union is built on a collaborative model that reflects women's typical styles of management. Independent workers help each other by creating a group to get lower rates on insurance, share knowledge, find work, achieve visibility, and take action. The group's Freelancers Insurance Company is a potential model for the safety net of the future.[6]

Using the Arts as a Platform for Change

Zeyba Rahman is a talented consultant who has organized major educational and cultural events, including the Fes Festivals of World Sacred Music in Morocco, which she opened up to local people, drawing a crowd of fifty thousand. She told me, "I have improvised my life, like jazz." Her career has spanned Wall Street and nonprofits but is now centered in her own multimedia arts company, Jungli Billi Productions, which builds community through the arts in many corners of the world.

The daughter of Afghani and Iranian parents, educated at a rigorous girls' boarding school in India, Zeyba says, "I was never reined in. I was free; my mind was unfettered." She has created her life's work in her own image and says, "We must make room for women to get around hard structures and embedded thinking with fluidity—like water. That is how change will happen."[7]

Opening Doors for Women Who Had Been Closed Out

Connie Evans is also a social entrepreneur. She has focused her life's work on creating opportunity for women who have been largely forgotten in the rush for big business, big profits, and big 401(k)s. As an African American woman with wide contacts in her community, she knew welfare mothers could be successful business owners if given a chance and a hand up. Connie created one of the very first successful microenterprise programs, the Chicago

Women's Self-Employment Project, which became a national model. She took her experience and expertise to the state and national levels, where she led policy change, and then the international level, spreading the word about how poor women are crucial economic players as they provide jobs for themselves and others, become role models for their children, and support their families.

Connie is now the president/CEO of the Association for Enterprise Opportunity, an organization for microenterprise groups. She has started companies and served as a consultant and on prestigious committees, including the Chicago Federal Reserve. But the centerpiece of her career has been opening the doors for women who have great potential but would otherwise have been closed out.[8]

Taking a Tiny Portfolio and Making Entire Systems Change

Noeleen Heyzer was the executive director of the United Nations Development Fund for Women (UNIFEM) when we last talked. A former banker, a consultant to Asian countries, and a women's organizer from Singapore via a PhD from Cambridge University, she is now UN undersecretary-general for Asia and the Pacific. Many organizations have a "women's office," but not many of them have been able to have widespread influence or leverage a tiny budget and an even tinier staff to create major institutional change. Noeleen led a team that did.

Under Noeleen's leadership, which included personal travel to war-torn and poor nations, UNIFEM gave hope to women and assistance to women's grassroots groups. Tackling democracy building and poverty in Africa, sex trafficking in Asia, and violence against women all over the world, Noeleen and her team showed what a small but dedicated and strategic group can do. It mobilized the larger and better-funded agencies of the UN to work with one hundred countries.[9]

Sara, Zeyba, Connie, Noeleen—and countless other women you know or have read about—started where they were to make a difference every day. The end point was not visible from the beginning. They took alternative paths to get where they wanted to go. Where do you want to go? What do you think must change for you to get there?

Takeaways

- With the Power of One you can make change happen.
- Personal satisfaction comes from being in charge of your own destiny as a change agent.
- Mother says, "When the door opens, go through."
- Think of yourself and preserve your positive energy.
- "Life is more than work" is a good motto.
- Organizing for change starts with asking: What do I want to change? How do I get there? Who can help me?

Tips on Changing from What Is to What Should Be

What do you think needs to change? When you identify your vision and jot it down— you have already taken the first step toward empowering yourself as a change agent. Here are three questions that define the first stages of moving forward as a transformative leader.

What is the need or problem you are trying to address?

Everyone's list will be different. Yours could include anything from your life—improving troublesome work practices, dealing with a difficult client, creating a women's committee, moving to a new job, electing new officers for an organization, increasing the number of special education teachers at your children's school. By defining the goal you can see what success would look like, even if it is some time away. Now you have an idea of where you want to go.

What steps will it take to get to the goal?

Creating change requires patience and planning, especially when it takes bringing other people along. Having a clear vision is critical, but often little changes are needed to add up to major outcomes. Going for the gold without small victories leads to discouragement (and often disaster).

Breaking difficult or long-range goals into simpler steps makes action easier and can clarify your thinking about who you need as part of your team. Also, small wins keep determination alive for the leader and spirits up for her team—and keep everybody on target.

Who can help (or might hinder) you in reaching your vision?

Leaders need teams, but they don't have to be large. Organizers know a small number of dedicated and energetic people can mobilize many others in wider and wider circles of influence. Think about who you know and could ask to be part of the solution. Do you know someone to talk with who could be an ally or provide a valuable insight before you make a decision? Asking for advice is a tried-and-true method of engaging people you don't know very well but would like to know better.

• • •

An enormous wave of change will begin if every person who reads this book or hears about it from a friend starts today with the Power of One. Next we'll discuss strategies to carry you further by making women's leadership more visible. Are you ready? Let's go.

7 Making Women's Power Visible

This chapter helps you stand up and speak out on women's needs and, even more important, women's power as a basis for economic growth and societal change. Use a gender lens and urge others to listen to women before they act. Amplifying women's voices creates a balance—usually we only hear men's views. Use sound research from independent sources to make the case for women-led answers.

Whether we like it or not, accountability for changing the status quo rests with women and the men who share our values. At least for the time being, we are missing the legal tools other societies have used to bring about balanced leadership. One thing we can do, though, is to bring women's strengths front and center by spotlighting women role models. Another is to raise questions about women's needs, strengths, and roles—and demand answers.

Women as Role Models

You can do this effectively through informal tactics today. Highlighting women's achievements—in a regular column in a company newsletter, a story in a community newspaper, a letter to the editor, or an awards event with publicity for the top women in your field—shows women as change agents who are essential to success. These efforts send an important subliminal message: great women's talent is everywhere around us, and it matters.

Even without a spotlight, we are role models for the women and girls—and the young men—behind us. We need to realize this and recognize the opportunities to reach out that are all around us.

I had an opportunity to be a role model when our then-ten-year-old granddaughter, Harper Jane Walker, asked me to visit with her class at Orangewood Elementary School in Fort Myers, Florida. Two excellent teachers expanded my visit to include about 150 boys and girls, who were seated on the floor of the library to hear me talk about being a woman leader.[1] This was a special morning for me, and the thank-you notes I received from the students showed that it had opened up horizons. Many of the girls and boys had learned for the first time about work at the top levels of government. Others had decided they wanted to become senators or run companies. My favorite note was from a girl who wrote, "I thought I would be a cosmetologist, now I think I will be a cosmetic surgeon."

Women's History Month in March can provide you with the ideal opportunity to speak at a local school or college career night and encourage other women in the community to do the same. An excellent point of contact would be one of the over two thousand women's studies or research centers in universities and community colleges. The Quick Fact Box provides talking points for putting your own career into a wider leadership context. More information is in the Resources section.

Raise Questions—It Matters

Women's voices must be heard saying what women need, want, and can offer. Even the most supportive men don't seem to get the differences gender can make unless women tell them. Often asking questions is the easiest (and least threatening) way to make your point. When you ask the right questions and provide relevant data and information, you are part of making positive change happen.

Quick Fact Box

- Three or more women on the board means higher profits. (Catalyst)

- Women have skills we need. More women graduate from every level of education than men of a similar age. (U.S. Census Bureau)

- More women leaders creates a competitive edge. We feel the pulse of eight out of ten U.S. consumers. (*Business Week*)

- Policies to value families rest on women, as the majority of voters and as elected leaders. (CAWP)

Asking questions seems difficult for many women, although I'm not sure why. When I speak before mixed audiences and reach the Q&A period, the initial flurry of hands is virtually all men. Sometimes I even have to ask if a woman has a question or comment. It opens the floodgates but leaves me wondering why women need a special invitation. Even if questioning doesn't come naturally to you, it's important to practice raising your voice effectively and encourage other women to do the same.

If you are an Outsider advocate, raising questions may mean being confrontational. Insiders, though, don't need to be and usually won't find it helpful. You don't have to pound the table or shout. Especially as one individual, you do need to be well informed, diplomatic, and unfailingly persistent. Do your homework, then ask pointed questions and follow up on the answers. When the answers are "We don't know," it is time to find out. (A note of caution: asking questions is not a substitute for Insiders organizing internally for change or Outside groups engaging in powerful advocacy.)

Sometimes one simple question suffices to start the process: Does this decision impact women differently than men, and how do we know? The more technical phrasing is to ask for "gender-disaggregated data." It is important for problems to be viewed in their entirety before solutions are developed. Women's impact statements and gender-responsive budgeting are two tools used in international work to challenge a time-honored but inaccurate automatic assumption of equal effects on men and women.

When asked this question about his proposal for rebuilding a country torn by war, one of my high-powered State Department contemporaries famously asked, "What difference does it make? Both men and women travel on the roads we build."

The answer, from women at the table who knew about the differential impacts of policies on women, was that while rebuilding roads and bridges would definitely provide jobs and opportunity, it would be insufficient to engage the female half of the population in recovery and growth. In the country under consideration, women and girls faced a terrific need for more education, for new wells so they would not have to walk miles daily to get water for their families, for basic health care, and for credit and other services to create jobs and future opportunity for both men and women. The disparate impacts of various investments were clear. Once gender impact was taken into account, it was possible to create a new and better plan to use the resources in a more equitable and balanced manner. The upshot of applying this "gender lens" was better progress toward the overall goal of economic and social development in a country devastated by war.

In another situation I was recently involved in, the question was raised too late. A well-known progressive economist was developing a major policy paper on poverty reduction for a group of foundations. When I saw the nearly final version, this comprehensive and well-reasoned document had statistics galore on issues and programs related to children, various minorities and ethnic groups, rural and urban problems, etc.

There were no specifics on something really important, though— women. This was a dramatic oversight, since single moms are the core of the adults in poverty in this country. The most recent Census Bureau data found that 8.9% of all men lived in poverty, 12.4% of all women—and 35.5% of single moms.[2]

When I asked the economist about the lack of focus on women, his response was enlightening: "Oh, if you had only been at the table when we developed the outline, it would have been included." He didn't seem to realize what he was missing. Without this focus, the writers could not really understand the problem they were trying to fix—and the decision makers who would use the report wouldn't understand it either. The report also missed potential solutions, including women-led solutions from international development and women's philanthropy, which have diminished poverty for entire families through self-sufficiency strategies, particularly for single mothers.

Sometimes it takes a lot more than one question! For example, here are a few good questions to ask to illuminate women's potential for increasing a company's success: Do our sales figures show a difference in reaching men and women? Do we have statistics based on gender so we can formulate the best sales strategy? Have we checked to see what our women customers want, or have we simply assumed that knowing what "people" want is sufficient? The default definition of "people" is almost always "men." For years auto manufacturers trumpeted cars on television with beautiful, buxom young models draped over their hoods. You haven't seen this approach for some time because they finally looked at who was buying their cars—more women than men.

One important goal of asking questions is to highlight women's strengths and the leadership value of women's experience. Women do continue to have a number of pressing problems that need attention, and we'll talk more about those in later chapters. Unless emphasis on these "women's issues" is balanced with emphasis on women's strengths, it can reinforce an impression of weaker, needy, and potentially dependent women. You can be part of balancing the story by showing the whole picture.

Here is a set of questions that can help: What is the talent base for the fast track in our company? Are we retaining the best women and men? Are women the primary clients or consumers for our products, and if so, is our record as a leader in creating a family-friendly workplace part of our marketing strategy? If the last question doesn't fit, perhaps this one will: Why are we stuck without a family-friendly workplace when other competitive companies are successfully structuring new ways to work—and finding them helpful in marketing to women consumers?

On a more personal level, perhaps you, your mother, or your daughter face tough medical problems and choices. Although the bodies of men and women are different, attention often has not been paid to how this affects health issues. For example, we now know women and men exhibit somewhat different heart attack symptoms, but for a long time only men's symptoms were listed as "what you should watch for."[3] Here the questions would be different: Were adequate research studies done on both men and women to determine the course of the disease and to find potential treatment techniques? Were the pharmaceutical products tested on women as well as men? Were the results the same? Are the screening requirements the same? Where are the women experts who are working to solve this problem, and what do they say?

Breast cancer, ovarian cancer, menopause, and other conditions that primarily or exclusively impact women were shrouded in darkness for many years. Have you ever wondered why the media, even medical and science publications, didn't uncover the lack of research on the size of these problems or the lack of research being done on them? Breast cancer has only recently stopped being a taboo subject. Women doctors, women scientists, and women's organizations started asking tough questions and realized the medical establishment had no real idea how many women were faced with this disease or what variations of treatment would be most successful. They gave visibility to the problem and championed research, new treatments, and routine prevention steps. When a cure is found, it will be due in no small measure to the women and their families who have marched in breast cancer awareness walks, worn pink ribbons to call attention to the problem, and never given up on questioning scientists and pressing legislators on the need for action. And it all started with asking questions.

Getting the Data You Need

It is difficult to notice the absence of something, but in mainstream media outlets, women's experience is often not present. A dearth of women's voices and faces in the media changes the contours of the debate by excluding women's experience from it. As in other elite institutions, many, many qualified women are working away in the media, but not many are at the top of the ladder.

Examples of this absence are legion. In October 2007, MSNBC's *Meet the Press* had an all-woman panel of prominent historians, journalists, and authors talking about how Hillary Clinton's campaign was changing the political dialogue. This was only the second all-woman panel in the history of this influential news show. A few years ago, the president and founder of The White House Project, Marie Wilson, pointed out that women made only 14% of guest appearances on the Sunday talk shows, which confer recognition on their guests as important national experts.[4] A lack of women at the microphone sends a self-reinforcing message that only men are experts. The percentage of women opinion columnists is stalled at less than 25% at the eight biggest syndicates; 90% of radio program directors are men; 85% of the general managers they report to are men; and most telling of all, only 3% of the media "clout" positions are held by women, which skews decisions on what is newsworthy. Excellent data on this topic are available through watchdog groups, such as the Women's Media Center, and networks for women in the media, such as the International Women's Media Foundation.[5]

Because of this dearth of women's voices, it's not possible to rely on the traditional media to cover the stories of importance to your life or the research that could help you make the case for attention to women's strong points or worries. What can you do? You need strong data. Fortunately, you don't have to start from scratch; independent research groups and foundations have conducted many excellent studies that will help build the foundation for your case. You may also need to ask for a study within your own organization to find out where you are and what needs to be done.

As we've discussed, the results of the study—whether of consumers, voters, employees, or some other group—should be gender disaggregated. Clearly, women, as half of the population, are not all the same—and neither are all men. However, we miss the similarities of women's priorities unless they are compared with men's, and making this comparison is still the exception, not the rule. Research is most valuable when it is also analyzed based on other critical factors, such as race or ethnicity, marriage status, and education.

Four types of studies that can give you ammunition are workforce studies, community studies, voter studies on how women and men vary in assessing important public priorities, and consumer studies determining who is buying what and why. Let's take them each in turn, then wrap up by reviewing another type of ammunition: investment power. More information is found in the Resources section.

Workforce Studies

The Families and Work Institute is your best source for national studies of the workforce over many years. In one particularly interesting project, the Institute collaborated with Catalyst on in-depth research into the drivers causing top leaders at global companies to feel engaged in their work. The researchers surveyed eight thousand senior and "pipeline" (next in line) executives around the world and found strong similarities in the drivers for top women and men: having a challenging job, a supportive workplace, a good fit between life on and off the job, and the opportunity for high achievement; being well compensated; and working at a company with high values. The primary difference was in how intensely women and men felt about these factors. Women valued a challenging job, a supportive workplace, and a good fit much more highly than men. Companies wanting to successfully recruit and retain talented senior management must recognize "one size fits all" simply won't work.[6]

A number of best-practice multinational corporations have done careful studies of their own workforces over many years, looking particularly at the distinctions between women and men. Companies like IBM, Marriott International, and Ernst and Young have led the way. While all of these studies are proprietary, the similarity of their results has been discussed in various meetings, and the programs these firms have developed for women's leadership, work supports, and flexibility have become industry standards. If you work for a major firm, the Human Resources Department can tell you if such data exist. If they don't (which is probable), you and other women can present the idea of doing a study to help track progress in your company. Women in smaller firms don't have this luxury, but if you own a business yourself, start today to see the needs of your own male and female employees.

Community Studies

A number of women's foundations, commissions, and statewide networks or alliances have done extensive studies on the situations of women and girls compared with those of men and boys in their states or localities. Chapter 5 described some of the results of such an effort in South Carolina. These studies can be extremely helpful in both visualizing the contributions of women to the local economy and throwing a spotlight on inadequate resources or programs to support the self-sufficiency efforts of women who have been forgotten or left out.

In 2003 the Washington Area Women's Foundation published the results of a two-year community effort to assess what was and wasn't happening for the 1.8 million women and girls in the Washington, D.C., region.[7] It looked at the disparities in women's lives by race, ethnicity, and county or part of the city, rating each jurisdiction against national trends. The report combined strong research findings with the results of eighteen community listening sessions to evaluate local issues by looking at the lives and experiences of girls and women. Anne Mosle, then heading the organization and now a vice president of the W. K. Kellogg Foundation, made clear to all of us working on the project, "Strong gender-disaggregated data are essential, and more of them need to be made available, but we need the voices of women to help us see how to interpret them."

The results of the study became the driver for multimillion-dollar programming over the next few years in a powerful partnership of the foundation, government, and business. The study pointed the way to where investments have the greatest impact: economic self-sufficiency for women-headed households, improved health outcomes for women of color and their children, and financial literacy as a baseline skill.

The study also concentrated the attention of community leaders on the assets women bring to the region's labor market—the high educational level of women in the metro area and the first-in-the-nation standing in the percentage of businesses that are owned by women. The foundation's approach—"look, listen, and then act"—and its balanced look at both womanpower and deficits on which community attention lagged gave it a powerful platform. A similar approach could be an idea for your community.

Voter Studies

Beginning with the 1980 election, women have been considered a potential voting bloc, and the "gender gap" has become a staple in political reporting. Since then, the difference in the voting patterns of men and women has given Democratic presidential candidates a 4% to 11% edge among women. The trend is not so much a value judgment by voters on specific individuals running for office as a reflection of how women see the positions of the two parties related to their priorities. Within groups of women, differences exist based on marital status, age, race and ethnicity, and party. However, women's hierarchy of concerns as a group and the weight or intensity of those concerns consistently differ significantly from those of men, regardless of their backgrounds and political persuasions.

A series of pioneering focus groups, state polls, and national surveys was launched in 1992 and repeated each presidential election cycle until 2000 with the goal of having *all* women's voices heard in the national campaigns. It was the first bipartisan and multicultural all-woman polling effort to capture women's ideas and priorities. Celinda Lake, head of Lake Research and known as the godmother of polling for and about women, led the study with Linda DiVall of American Viewpoint. Over the eight years, women consistently spoke about economic issues in terms of Main Street and family economic security, not Wall Street.

This finding is consistent with a more general observation about the approaches of men and women voters. In many subtle ways women voters use inductive logic, reasoning from a series of individual examples of people and situations they know about to prioritize what they think is important for the country (such as more early education programs so kids do better in school). Men voters are more likely to use deductive reasoning, starting with a general premise (such as "taxes are too high" or "America must be a

Takeaways

- Showing the positive benefits of more women leaders is our task.
- The starting point is asking pointed questions about impact—until you get answers.
- Raising your voice to make the case requires good solid data on both men and women.
- The base for a better future is women's strength—as employees, consumers, voters, and investors.
- Unless women's concerns are visible, they can't be addressed. Unless our strengths are visible, we can't move ahead.

dominant military power"), which leads to a different set of priorities. Both inductive and deductive reasoning are legitimate and credible, but deductive reasoning has overwhelmingly dominated government policy making.

Over decades, and with considerable passion, women have placed health care, equal pay, jobs, and flexible work arrangements at the top of their list of issues needing attention. These pocketbook concerns revolve around time and money and involve family economic security and control over their multifaceted lives. Women are proud of their hard work and contributions but think it is high time for government and employers to be active partners with them in achieving the economic security they seek. Men have generally agreed that the four issues of greatest concern to women are important. However, they have been much less passionate about them and more prone to prioritize taxes, national economic issues, and national security. Accordingly, it is these issues that have dominated our political conversation.[8]

Studies of men and women voters have been continued by other organizations, such as Women's Voices, Women Vote, which works to improve the electoral and policy engagement of unmarried women. This is the fastest-growing demographic in the country: 47% of American women are unmarried. In the past their views were seldom heard, and their concerns were not prominent in political campaigns. Economic security is their primary interest, since four in ten single women earn less than $30,000 per year.[9]

Consumer Studies

This is a consumer-driven economy. Although women lose close to a quarter of earned income due to the gender wage gap, women's buying power has increased to 80% of the total as more women head households, live longer, work more hours, and work their way up the ladder—not to mention make a majority of the buying decisions in families even when men are present.[10]

If your company markets consumer products, try a basic tutorial like this one by Andrea Learned to help management realize women are not just a niche market: "If your business generates $100 million a year and women purchase or influence [the purchase of] 80% of all of your goods and services, women are an $80 million factor in your business." Learned suggests, "Work the numbers into a visual comparison to give . . . a clear, and dramatic, picture of the role women play in your current success and future growth."[11] Presenting data like these raise the visibility of women's power—and of your leadership. While consumer studies done by individual companies are closely guarded secrets, industry-wide data and outside research can be used to make the case for conducting such studies at your company.

The financial sector has been the leader in realizing it needs to learn how to reach women consumers effectively. A clear business imperative got its attention: by 2010 women are expected to control 60% of the wealth in the United States. Allianz Life commissioned a survey to learn more about how and why women invest for the future. It found that women saw financial security and freedom as fifteen to twenty times as important as money-related status or respect. Yet 90% of women surveyed felt "only somewhat" or "not at all" financially secure—even women who earned more than $100,000 per year. Although women's earning power is on the rise, about half in the survey worried about becoming impoverished.[12] Many financial firms are using data like these to change their marketing

---

This Week I Will . . .

✔ Start to ask about how women clients or consumers fit into the work my organization does and whether we have data on that.

✔ Check out whether our community foundation or women's fund has done a report on the status of women locally to see how our strengths and needs might be made more visible.

✔ Always ask "Why not?" if my organization doesn't have the answers on the similarities and differences between men and women.

---

strategies and speak directly to women investors through financial seminars, targeted advertising, and an increase in the number of women brokers. This is another case where increasing personal confidence is justified.

Despite women's fears, the latest studies should be empowering: they show women investors make fewer mistakes than men. A Merrill Lynch study stated, "It may fall short of being an actual genetic defect, but whatever it is about men that prevents them from asking for driving directions apparently impairs their investing abilities as well, at least as compared to women." Women had more diverse portfolios, did more extensive research—based more on expert opinion and less on stock tips from friends—and were less likely to act on emotion. Men were much more likely to cite their own mistakes as caused by greed, overconfidence, and impatience.[13] This sounds like an argument for more women in financial leadership to me.

Investment Power

If you work at or own shares in a publicly held company, you have another tool at your disposal. These companies need to keep their stockholders happy and continuing to invest in the corporation. Make sure the front office knows that gender equality as an investment concept is growing.

Some mutual funds invest only in financially successful and socially responsible companies that meet specified economic, environmental, and social and governance criteria. Socially responsible investing (SRI) is based on a belief that sustainable firms will do the best in the long run. Women are the primary SRI investors.

A newer SRI premise is that companies that advance, empower, and invest in women will be stronger, more sustainable, and more profitable in the long run. In 2004, the Calvert Funds and UNIFEM unveiled a global corporate code of conduct. The Calvert Women's Principles dealt with all aspects of corporate practice intersecting women's employment, from reporting and transparency to income, health and safety, community engagement, management and governance, training and professional development, and supply chain and marketing.[14] This advance turns the tables on the old message that women need to fix ourselves to fit into a man's world. Instead, using the talents and experiences of women wisely at all levels of a corporation creates a competitive edge, enhancing long-term success and increasing shareholder value.

In late 2007, Pax World, the country's oldest SRI firm, took a big step forward and launched the only mutual fund in the country with a women's dimension.[15] Its Women's Equity Fund (WEF) invests only in firms with good potential for long-term sustainability *because* they meet additional criteria of having strong women's leadership (board and management), treating women decently in their advertising, and dealing with women employees and suppliers equitably and with respect. Pax is involved in shareholder activism on issues like trafficking and is working with the International Finance Corporation, the private-sector investment arm of the World Bank, to develop a set of gender investment indexes.[16]

This is a development worth sharing with investors who are interested in women's advancement—and with men leading public companies who have never thought about it. Does your company want its stock to be purchased by these mutual funds? If shareholders with these values start asking questions, how will it be able to respond?

• • •

You now have leads on solid independent research data on the consumer, voting, and financial strength women bring to companies and communities.

So raise your voice—and use a gender lens—to inform decisions and help make progress toward having enough women at the power tables to add the "difference that 'difference' makes." Help make women's strengths, as well as concerns, transparent enough so they can't be ignored by CEOs, investors, or politicians, and create the momentum to address problems that were previously invisible.

We've covered two stops on your leadership journey. Next let's look at how we can lift other women up with us as we climb—and get to our goals faster.

8 Lifting as We Climb

Here are some additional ways you can personally help other women advance and create positive change in organizations to make it easier. "Lifting as we climb" was the motto of the National Association of Colored Women at the end of the 19th century and is still great advice today. Each of us can live this ideal. The effect doubles when we join together to support each other and create win-win solutions that work for everyone and significantly help women.

"If you want to go fast, go alone; if you want to go far, go together." This African proverb, often quoted by financier Warren Buffett, has been borne out by new and exciting research about women leaders. This chapter looks at the nature of women's leadership with particular attention to the importance of connecting and engaging, and explores some issues for which these approaches can help create win-win solutions.

"Each One, Reach One" by Mentoring

One form of engaging, mentoring, is the next step up from being a role model. For every woman who has made it over an old barrier, many energetic, talented women are looking for advice and assistance.

Mentoring is no mystery. Indeed, it comes naturally to women, despite some popular stereotypes to the contrary. Most of the readers of this book have a mutually supportive group of women in their lives—in the PTA, at a workout studio, at a child care cooperative, in the neighborhood, in the family. You and your friends aren't catty, jealous, judgmental, or bitchy—yet these images of women are cited as proof "women can't work together." My own experience in life is that women support each other, and I've gotten a great deal of strength and sustenance from helping other women and having women mentor me. So let's zero in on how you can be a mentor to help lift someone up.

A few terrific formal mentoring programs exist in forward-leaning companies or organizations that are highly focused on talent management. Occasionally graduate programs and women's leadership programs match faculty mentors with students to help women with the tough climb in an environment where the top leadership is overwhelmingly male. Entrepreneurial programs exist to connect newcomers with successful businesswomen in person or online. Unfortunately, there are not nearly enough of these programs.

A number of women's organizations facilitate international peer-to-peer mentoring. For example, the Vital Voices Global Partnership seeks to increase the capacity and outside credibility of emerging women leaders around the world through training and connections to U.S. women mentors. The U.S. women, who come from every profession, gain a more international viewpoint. Founder Melanne Verveer envisioned Vital Voices as a way for women to give back together by mentoring and help create a new world where women are full partners. This is a successful model you could bring home, starting small and growing gradually in a business, an organization, or a community.

Far more common than formal mentoring is informal mentoring, where the mentor can offer some advice, share a bit of knowledge, or transfer what she or he has learned. This responsibility goes along with having a seat at the table. Your expertise or experience—whatever it is—can be valuable to someone else. And someone else's can be equally valuable to you. You can be (or have) a mentor at any age or stage of life. If you are a midcareer woman, look not only for senior women as mentors but for younger women who can expand your worldview. Look horizontally, too (inside or outside of where you work), and don't rule out male mentors.

Generally, informal mentoring can be initiated either by the person seeking advice or by the mentor. An informal mentoring relationship often begins over a cup of coffee when someone asks for advice or looks to you for encouragement. Frequently the first question asked is more personal—about the story of your career (often how to integrate a full life with the job) or whether to return to school (and in what program)—rather than about a specific work-related problem. As in any other relationship, trust must build. Keep in touch and be available—as close as the phone or e-mail.

You don't have to wait for someone to come to you, though. You can actively look for creative women who are ready and motivated to move up and need a hand. Ask them to join you and talk about their career potential—maybe you can link them up with someone in your network who could be helpful to them. Take the initiative to recommend a talented woman to others who are making a decision to add someone to a committee, nominate a candidate, or hire a new staffer.

If there is no opportunity to mentor someone at work, how about working with college women or the Girl Scouts or another youth group? What about your own circle? Do you have a sister, a niece, or a cousin, or does a friend or neighbor have a daughter, who could learn from you—or just needs to know she has abundant potential? Women's foundations in some cities have developed ways to match up professional women who have "made it" with grassroots leaders who are working one-on-one to help women and girls become self-sufficient and successful. Check the Resources section to connect to the Women's Funding Network.

Sometimes you are mentoring without knowing it. In your workplace, are you a source of inspiration or knowledge for other women? Have you taken a young woman or girl under your wing to show her the ropes? How about serving as a coach or being a sounding board for your friend's career? Keep it up and expand your reach—you are already mentoring, even if you don't know your own impact. Once at a Salzburg Global Seminar, a young, dynamic academic dean from the National Taiwan University left me a note saying, "Thank you for the important advice you gave me about how to reframe my issue in Taiwan just within the split second in the hallway the other day." This was a bit of speed-mentoring I didn't know I had done.

Here is another idea: Make it a habit to quietly reach out and give constructive advice or encouragement to a woman in your life who has done something deserving of mention—whether at work, at church, or in the neighborhood. If she is acting like a leader, tell her so. She might not recognize it herself, and her self-confidence will be raised. These simple steps count a lot. You can make a difference with a simple compliment or congratulatory note.

The joy of "each one, reach one" also contributes to the 30% Solution. When you take the time to mentor another woman or girl, the way is easier for her than it has been for you. It is a great way to give back.

Mentoring also has a subtler benefit for women's advancement. Some women on the way up have stayed aloof from helping others and simply become "one of the boys." In the late '70s, Professor Rosabeth Moss Kanter at Harvard Business School wrote that women who were in "skewed working groups" (at most 15% women) felt like outsiders who were required to conform to dominant male norms and blend into male culture. Women have come a long way in the last thirty years in terms of independence, confidence, and experience, but we still have work to do to break that pattern.[1] By mentoring, you can help.

You Benefit, Too

When you reach out to a woman or girl who is looking for advice and counsel, you often gain as much as you give—or more. One-on-one interactions helping someone else succeed improve your ability to visualize how to be successful yourself. You also end up modeling positive behavior and developing more structured plans, which can position you to be seen as a leader by others. In addition, leadership is all about empowering others, not doing everything yourself. Making a conscious effort to mentor will serve you well as a leader and help you avoid feeling isolated or toppling into the martyrdom pit of trying to do it all.

This Week I Will . . .

✔ Informally mentor another woman at work to pass on what I had to learn in the "school of hard knocks."

✔ Offer to help a younger woman or girl realize her dreams by finding the time to write a recommendation letter.

✔ Find an opportunity to provide constructive advice or a compliment to a woman colleague with leadership potential.

✔ Invest time in helping woman-to-woman to give me energy to "keep on keeping on."

Having a sense of satisfaction in "passing it on" also reinforces you as a leader. Sometimes you will not know you made a difference until much later, when you hear that a woman you mentored is doing wonderful work and is recognized as a fine leader in her field. You can look back and feel great about having had a small part in her journey. A teacher I know once mentored a talented but uncertain young woman and then lost track of her. Recently my friend heard on the grapevine that she is the spark and vice principal of a rural school making strides for excellence in a deeply impoverished area. The good news buoyed my teacher friend as well.

Some new and exciting research about women leaders shows that linking, connecting, and engaging are critical elements to sustain success. As we discussed earlier, the McKinsey Leadership Project has identified "centered leadership" as the approach that best helps women navigate the difficult path leading upward. Centered leadership enhances the ability and energy level of women like you to "stay the leadership course" and thrive. We discussed three of its five characteristics (finding meaning in your work, managing your energy level, and framing situations positively) in Chapter 6. The final two are:

Connecting—"People with strong networks and good mentors enjoy more promotions, higher pay, and greater career satisfaction. They feel a sense of belonging, which makes their lives meaningful."[2]

Engaging—Helping others succeed and working together to make change happen provide job satisfaction.

The elements of centered leadership reaffirm the two-way benefits of mentoring. Both giving and receiving mentoring can help you thrive and enjoy life as a leader. Think about this when your first instinct is that time spent mentoring is time away from your work. I have found mentoring relationships—both up and down the career ladder and horizontally—give me energy and purpose. In fact, mentoring and personal involvement in making change are essential ingredients for a satisfying leadership career.

Beyond Mentoring: Build Collective Strength to Bring More Women Up

One-on-one mentoring means a lot, but often more is needed. You can learn from the experiences of women in government and leading corporations who have come together to promote progress for more women. Even a few women in an organization or at the top of a profession can move seemingly immovable systems by working in concert.

We can thank some of the earliest national women's commissions—composed of prominent citizens and top governmental officials—for opening opportunity. The first Presidential Commission on the Status of Women was established in 1960 by President John F. Kennedy and chaired by Eleanor Roosevelt. Since then, commissions at the state and national level have waxed and waned.

Often it is necessary to reinvent such structures to keep them true to the original goals, but we can't do without them if we want to achieve balanced leadership. Before President Obama created the White House Council on Women and Girls in March 2009, the most recent federal effort was the very successful President's Inter-Agency Advisory Council on Women, set up by President Bill Clinton to assure coordinated government-wide action to implement the Beijing Platform for Action. Unfortunately, President George W. Bush discontinued all the presidential-level initiatives, and progress languished.

President Obama's new White House Council includes the heads of all federal agencies, whether men or women. This is the highest-level group addressing gender impact in the history of the country and brings the United States more closely into line with many other countries that have a direct line from the president or prime minister to the women's ministry.[3] When he created the council, Obama identified women's talents as a crucial but underutilized resource for very difficult economic times, pointing specifically to the pay gap and the leadership gap as critical issues.[4]

Top-level women's committees, councils, commissions, or caucuses that have the primary goal of opening up the system and report directly to the top boss exist in many professional organizations, companies, universities, legislatures, and local governments. They are of all types and have various levels of impact. Some are formed from the bottom up to bring concerns to management's attention. Others are created from the top down to provide insight on solving particular problems. Some meet simply to meet and have virtually no authority or agenda. Many are political footballs whose fate depends on which political party holds the mayor's or governor's office or on whether they serve the philosophical or partisan interests of the current leadership. Nevertheless, such groups can serve as catalysts for change and concerted voices for advancing women.

In Congress and most state legislatures, Insider women's caucuses and Outsider coalitions have been able to work collectively across party lines to advance women. They have had to steer away from anything tagged as an abortion issue, though, which has been a challenge. The fights over women's reproductive rights have raged at both the state and the national level for almost fifty years and have held back other gains, with opponents tying every issue to abortion. My longtime colleague Judith Lichtman, founder of the National Partnership for Women and Families (a leading advocate for women in Washington since 1971), explains, "The best way to divide our coalition working for women's equality was to focus on the need to defend abortion rights. When we thought we were working on education, it turned out we were forced to defend reproductive rights.

The same defensive battles occupied us on employment and justice issues, making it harder to make the gains women need."[5]

Groups can move faster through coordinated action at both state and national levels. Often state laws have become models and created momentum for national legislation. For example, led by women's legislative caucuses in partnership with advocacy coalitions, thirty states passed family and medical leave (FMLA) legislation before Congress did. The congressional fight took eight years, and President George H. W. Bush vetoed the law twice. It was the first piece of legislation signed into law by President Clinton. During those eight years, whether you had any protection from losing a job because of a family emergency depended on what state you lived in.

A new cycle has started now, with states moving to pass *paid* family leave bills providing essential protection for earnings. New Jersey, California, and Washington State are in the forefront. The movement has been led by women's legislative caucuses and women governors on the Inside and advocates on the Outside. (We'll discuss family leave further below and in Chapter 10.)

Private-sector women's committees have also had positive impacts. For example, JPMorgan Chase, under the leadership of CFO Dina Dublon, brought together an advisory group of senior women from various parts of the company when it faced a big and expensive problem: the brain drain resulting from a rapid turnover of talented women. The group found that the high cost of recruitment and training far outweighed the costs of a program of mentoring and the provision of services women were looking for to allow them to compete equally. In time those services came to include increased flexibility, an on-site child care center, and nationwide emergency child care services, which continue today. When I talked with the women at this financial giant, nine women were on the corporate executive committee—quite a difference from a few years ago, when women could not even be branch managers. Unfortunately, it didn't last. Now the committee has four women.

These stories illustrate the power of women working together to make changes that are good for all. Unfortunately, they also show how progress for women can regress or progress with a change in the top executive, whether president or CEO. The changing priorities are yet one more reason to have more women at the top to keep the focus on opening opportunity.

With at least a sprinkling of women moving up the ladder everywhere, models like these can help you change your organization, too. Most of these groups have lasting positive effects on organizational practices. Don't despair if you need to renew or restart such a group—it is worth your effort. As Margaret Mead said, "Never doubt that a small group of thoughtful citizens can change the world. Indeed, it is the only thing that ever has."

Promote Change That Works for Everyone (and Levels the Playing Field)

Until we have a critical mass of women at the policy table, problems identified as relating just to women won't seem anywhere near as important as "real" issues related to the success of the enterprise, no matter how important they are to you (or, for that matter, to the enterprise). Until we reach that critical mass, to drive change on issues like child care, family leave, workplace flexibility, and moving women up, you need to be strategic. It's crucial to make one point loud and clear: while it may be women who are most interested in seeing progress, women who lead the charge, and women who mobilize to make it happen, *everyone will benefit*. Women-led solutions produce wide gains for our society *and* make it easier for women to rise. Specific benefits of such changes are described throughout this book.

We can learn from African women activists, who present the need for change in terms of freeing up the strengths of women to set a new agenda and create a better future. You don't hear debates about discrimination against women—despite the devastating facts. Instead their mantra is about hope and optimism. They say, "When women flourish, families flourish. When families flourish, so do communities and nations." These courageous women have successfully organized in impoverished countries like Liberia, which now has its first woman president.

Here, too, changing today's reality requires all of us to leave behind victim talk, negative or conspiratorial expectations, and the defensiveness that Outsiders often feel. In any event, fewer and fewer of the barriers in our way are the result of a determined conspiracy trying to keep women down.

Change Outdated Ways of Doing Business

Many businesses maintain working conditions and ways of operating that were designed for a different time and workforce. They have created needless hurdles to women's advancement. Some women are champion hurdlers and get over the barriers easily, but many more will only have a real chance to reach the top when the barriers fall. The key to demolishing them is to realize (and help others realize) they don't just hamper women—they hinder organizations from reaching their goals. When these old traditions are replaced by newer ideas proved to yield better results, your company will be more profitable, you (and other employees) can do a better job—and more women will climb the career ladder.

Here's how it works. Step away for a minute from a problem you know is constraining you or other women. Now reframe it and articulate a win-win solution that produces gains *other than* for women. This might take some research, but women will win when you can show how everyone will win. As a side benefit, you will be more likely to be seen as an emerging leader. Offering a solution to improve productivity, competitiveness, and economic growth is the act of an Insider—a mainstream problem solver, a smart businessperson—not an Outsider pleading for special treatment.

For example, take the need for family leave. Activists have learned to frame this (quite accurately) as a family issue affecting all working people. Here's the best case: family leave policies increase employees' engagement and loyalty while decreasing the costs of absenteeism and turnover. While I am drawn to working on family leave because it reinforces compassion and caring, focusing on preventing home concerns from diminishing productivity works better as an argument. It keeps family leave from seeming like a special privilege demanded by or benefiting only women. In reality, family leave is a women-led change that will help everyone.

Two other problem areas involve flexibility and contracting. Rigid hours and places of work make responsibly balancing work and family very difficult without a spouse at home. They are also counterproductive for business success. Closed systems of contracting prevent many women-owned businesses from getting a piece of the action. They also keep companies buying goods and services from getting better deals. Let's look in more detail at job rigidity and closed contracting. This time, we'll put them into a positive business frame based on the latest research findings.

Example One: Improve Bottom-Line Performance by Increasing Flexibility

It's time for each of us—wherever we are—to push for increasing flexibility to improve productivity. Although flexibility has been a top concern of working women and many men for decades, the latest far-reaching study by the Families and Work Institute found little momentum toward increased flexibility. The number of employers allowing *some* employees to move from full time to part time and back while remaining in the same position dropped 10% from 1998 to 2008, although the number allowing at least *some* employees to periodically change their start or departure time increased 9%.[6] "Some" is an important qualifier here. Other studies have shown that the further down the career ladder you go, the more important flexibility is to employees—but the less likely they are to have it. Flexibility is available only to a very tiny percentage of employees in small to medium-sized firms. It is likelier in firms with more women and minorities in top positions, according to the Families and Work Institute study.

Studies by Corporate Voices for Working Families (CVWF) show that corporate officers erroneously see flexibility as an option to meet women's special needs rather than a useful practice to improve performance. This attitude fences us in.

Flexibility Quiz

How much flexibility do you have now?

- Working four longer days, not five short ones, to cut down on transportation time—more for you, kids, school, or community.

- Changing your starting or ending time to manage school, commuting, second job, or family responsibilities.

- Taking a sabbatical to freshen your outlook or skills.

- Telecommuting or working from home to stay with a sick child, wait for a repairman—or just concentrate.

Who makes the decisions? What data do you need? Who is the best person who already works flexibly and can help you create a new policy? (Hint: Look up to the top levels for new parents.)

The traditional nine-to-five day—with rush hours on both ends and no match to school hours—is not very useful anymore. When the workday and workweek are both long and inflexible, many women—and, increasingly, men—have a hard time finding ways to meet family, work, and community responsibilities. The stress level climbs, and something has to give. Often women decide not to move up the ladder where they are, or even to stay there. Flexibility in the hours and places work gets done clears the way for a better quality of life immediately and makes it possible for both men and women with families to move up and manage all the intersecting spheres of life. It's true that these changes are especially important for women because we still carry more family responsibilities, but they benefit men and the family pocketbook as well—not to mention the carbon footprint.

Is your employer unreceptive to such "lifestyle" arguments? Try this one: Solid studies show rigid hours are not the best way to do business.[7] Different approaches have been proved to increase productivity, decrease turnover, and save employers money. As you can see from the Flexibility Quiz, lots of creative ways exist to achieve these goals. Information and studies are available to help you make the case.

CVWF is one of the best groups making this case. Led by CEO Donna Klein, long a leader in the work/life field, CVWF is a corporate membership organization that seeks to improve public policy on working families. Its extensive research shows that telecommuting and flexible schedules improve the bottom line by increasing retention and engagement in the company.[8]

A focus group with top corporate women on the board of CVWF made it clear that flexibility is an essential tool to attract and retain talent. One executive had everyone agreeing when she said, "Men and women who are Gen Yers are looking to restructure the whole work/life balance for both sexes. The best ones say, 'I don't want to give up my family or my life for the trappings of success.'"[9]

A bright Gen Y woman talked to me after a recent speech. Echoing many others, she said, "I turned down a promotion in my company because it meant working for a boss who was unbending on the flexibility I needed with a young family and a husband who also traveled." She was on the management fast track of this Fortune 100 firm, which had good policies on paper but not in practice. She now has tremendous loyalty and commitment to her new company in the same industry, a firm that is attracting bright people by being extremely flexible. She is doing the same work from home, happier and more productive.

So here's the argument to present wherever you work. Expanded flexibility policies help recruit and retain the best employees; improve human capital outcomes by improving engagement in the work and the company; and improve financial performance (operational and business outcomes) by raising productivity and lowering turnover and training costs. Every successful company needs to excel in exactly these areas. And will women benefit, too? Of course!

Example Two: Opening Up Contracting for Women-Owned Businesses Creates Jobs

Women make most consumer decisions, whether for themselves, their own companies, or their employers. Are you or any of your friends a small-business owner, or the person responsible for purchasing for your company, school district, or local government, or an executive involved in setting top-level policy on purchasing? If so, having women-owned small businesses as part of your supply chain for goods and services is a great opportunity for you to get good deals and spur job development.

Contracting for goods or supplies is a huge, lucrative business—and a very traditional one where "old boys' networks" are often the primary route to being asked to bid. Supplier diversity opens the door for women-owned businesses to compete and brings multiple benefits for them, your organization, and the community.

The federal government, which is the largest purchaser of goods and products, has promised but failed to open market access wide. Only about 3% of all contracts are going to women-owned firms, despite a decades-old goal of 5%, because no accountability exists. Some of the largest U.S. corporations have implemented supplier diversity programs and are reaping clear rewards—outstanding products and services at good prices. Your company or organization could do the same.

Women's entrepreneurship has been identified as one of the most useful strategies to grow local economies by the Organisation for Economic Cooperation and Development (OECD), based in Paris and made up of the industrialized countries of the world. Virginia Littlejohn, chair of Quantum Leaps, Inc., a nonprofit global accelerator of women's entrepreneurship, has been the leader in getting this important international group to recognize the overarching importance of women-owned businesses to economic growth. She said, "I remember thinking it would take forever if every country on its own has to plant the idea. OECD can be the multicountry fast track and accelerate progress with policy, transfer of ideas, and face-to-face meetings."[10]

Opening the closed doors for women-owned businesses is good business for everyone at competitive prices. It also helps women thrive. In my experience, these companies have a proven track record of leadership in workplace flexibility. "Making a difference" is a common reason for being in business, and many of the owners are also community leaders.

•   •   •

We can reach a critical mass of empowered women more quickly and easily when each of us promotes women-led win-win solutions like those given above. Lifting as we climb can become a way of life for you. The next chapter will help you put a simple strategy into play to wedge the door further open.

9 Wedging the Door Open

Your next step will include an amazingly simple set of strategies to get women like yourself on the fast track to leadership positions. A strong virtual circle begins when great candidates have real opportunity to compete. When we elect more women to office, they wedge the door open for more women in top appointed positions and for better policies. The same holds true in business. Having more women in executive suites and on boards opens opportunities for others. You can start by yourself and then work to change the ground rules with the "women in every pool" plan, so more women can lead the way.

Now we've laid the groundwork for women moving up. How can we make sure we don't backslide when the next CEO, governor, or boss doesn't have women's advancement as a priority? The powerful bottom-line benefits of expanding women's leadership possibilities shouldn't be lost. We know just making the case for balanced leadership does not provide enough impetus to give many women a chance. Progress can stall, and inertia sets in. Simply waiting for a better atmosphere is not an option, and one-at-a-time progress is pretty glacial. We need effective strategies to build momentum and leap forward.

Are you tired of hearing that no women "made the cut" for a position when you are pretty sure no women were actually considered? Let's look at some strategies to make sure women like you will be actively recruited, be considered, and have a good chance to be chosen for leadership positions. We'll start with some things you can do right away, then raise our sights to some interesting, more formal models that have been shown to work.

Women in Every Pool of Finalists for Everything!

No woman can be chosen for a job, a promotion, a nomination for public office, a seat on a board of directors, or a slot in a training program unless women are in the pool of finalists. Having women as finalists does not guarantee success for any one woman—nor should it. However, we won't get much closer to the 30% Solution until we wedge the door open.

Again, change starts with asking questions and taking steps yourself. Do you have a say in hiring or promoting staff in your own company, organization, or department? If so, make sure women are contenders—even if you have to go out and find candidates yourself. If you are a business owner or senior staff member, move to make "a woman in every pool" a corporate policy. If you are on the board of a professional or community organization, require a policy to be put into place.

Take a look at current personnel policies and practices in your company. Watch for processes that seem to offer equal opportunity but have different impacts on men and women. For example, civil service rules in many places give bonus points on exams to veterans or volunteer firefighters. On their face these practices appear fair, rewarding sacrifices made to protect all of us. However, when only the top three scorers can be considered, such a policy shrinks women's chances to compete, since far fewer women are veterans or volunteers for the fire department. Fairness would mean considering the top three candidates before bonus points are awarded, plus any other candidates who make the grade by virtue of their extra points. At most this means a few more prospective people to interview, and it is much more likely that at least one woman will be in the pool.

If your company has a standard honoring diversity or is required to meet federal equal opportunity guidelines as a contractor, this will help

Thinking in a New Way

A CEO friend put the "women in every pool" idea into effect in her organization. She introduced a formal personnel policy, and managers were held accountable and evaluated on their follow-through.

This simple step allowed many more opportunities for talented women to be considered and, over time, changed the leadership mix at the top.

She said, "It is still true for most women, if they have a good enough resume to be considered for the job, they are often better qualified than the men since they had to work harder to get to this point. But you won't know that unless they have a chance to compete in the finals."

you raise the need for a policy of "women in every pool." Such a policy will change the outcomes over time, especially if hiring authorities are held accountable. If not, you and your colleagues have work to do!

Remember, being sure a full field of the best competitors for the job will actually be considered is not favoritism or reverse discrimination. No one benefits on the bottom line if good talent is kept out of the running by old-think or downright prejudice questioning the existence of equally qualified women. When managers and supervisors are charged with looking hard to complete the pool as part of their responsibility—and evaluated on their performance—more women move up, and we get closer to leadership balance.

Here are some ways you can expand on this idea. If you are putting together a meeting or a panel presentation, ask yourself, "Are a significant number of women represented?" As a decision maker, I've had great success with simply requiring the selection of an equal number of men and women to attend top-level meetings. This changes the customary dialogue and gives women as well as men a platform for increasing their skills. The Center for Policy Alternatives, which I headed, sponsored the Flemming Fellows Leadership Institute for state elected leaders, and the selection committee chose one-half men and one-half women for each class after a highly competitive national process.

In another example, the planning committee for a series of international conferences of progressive think tanks asked all participating organizations to bring equal numbers of men and women to the table. Most complied, and the gender balance added new substance. The outcomes mirrored those of the Flemming Fellows leadership program in terms of networking, consideration of issues, and approaches to building consensus. The evaluations were overwhelmingly positive, primarily because of the mix of people at the table.

You might not be in a position yet to require equal representation, but you can be effective in other ways. Again, asking questions like "Where are the women?" may start the process. You can also suggest good places to look for qualified women candidates. Or you might volunteer for a nominating committee, which gains you wider contacts as well as the experience of being part of the process. As a member of a search committee for a board or management position in a nonprofit agency or a company, you can suggest drafting a policy statement about the importance of diversity and inclusion in the search process and, particularly, in the presentation of final candidates.

If you are an investor, watch for and support shareholder activism by socially responsible investment firms that are looking at not only the quality but also the gender composition of top management in the companies in their portfolios. These efforts are gaining steam. Several years ago, the Calvert Funds CEO, Barbara Krumsiek, wrote to the companies in Calvert's investment portfolio that had no, or only a few, women on their boards. She recommended the creation of new nominating committee policies to require women finalists in any group being considered for appointment to the board. Many companies responded positively to this voluntary proposal since it came from an investment firm.[1] The Pax World Women's Equity Fund goes further, considering gender composition of the board and management and other gender screening criteria when deciding which firms to invest in.

The Need for Diversity Goals and Benchmarks

Most successful enterprises use the smart management practice of engaging in extensive strategic planning to establish benchmarks and metrics to check progress on meeting goals. Seldom do those targets deal with expanding the leadership at the top. However, some companies and countries have realized how diverse leadership including women brings strength in a multicultural, globalized world, where more and more women are well educated and employed, create jobs, and manage wealth. They publicly set goals. For example, top leaders in Chile and Spain, elected as "change candidates," have established 50:50 cabinets.

Setting goals or timetables is often highly controversial, as if opening opportunity for women—often the best candidates—somehow cheats men of their rightful places. Just mentioning that more than one hundred other countries have developed formal processes to assure a critical mass of women at government power tables causes a few people to come up after my remarks and "take me on." Here is the most frequent statement from women: "I want to be promoted on my own merits, not to meet a quota."

Step back for a few minutes from political rhetoric and think about the challenge we face without tools such as benchmarks or goals. The pipeline theory that women would "naturally" move into leadership when enough of us came up through the ranks has sprung a leak. When, despite the enormous number of highly educated and experienced women, at least 95% of executives at the vice president level and above at Fortune 1500 companies are men, the system remains pretty tightly closed.[2]

A lot of talent will continue to be locked out or underutilized unless we find the pressure points to convince—or require—those who benefit from the current system to throw open the doors. Positive policies are needed in every field to make the inclusion of viable women candidates a must, with no excuses allowed. Opening the process doesn't and shouldn't mean women are guaranteed particular positions. It should mean real opportunity exists to compete, and competition should be about getting the best person for the job.

The nature of many male-only corporate suites and boardrooms leads to chummy, comfortable selections from a narrow band of people only one degree separated from those already present. It is "who you know, not what you know." The business pages are full of stories about executive compensation committees approving sky-high salaries and "golden parachutes" regardless of firm profitability. Everyone seems surprised that these committees are full of lifetime friendly, cozy relationships. All too often, in hiring someone to sit at the power table, the boss wants to personally vet the candidate through someone he (and it is almost always "he") knows.

Fairly early in my career, I saw this custom in action in a way that actually benefited me. The same episode, though, taught me firsthand about the benefits of benchmarks. I was chosen as a "diversity fellow" for a wonderful executive seminar at the Aspen Institute. There was a requirement that one woman (me) and one person of color (an African American man) be added to the usual group of top executives (as in real life, these were all white men). I've always been grateful for the opportunity. Did the fact I was chosen to meet a quota lessen the importance of the experience for me? No. Would I have been present without this requirement? No. Was it hard? Yes.

I learned so much from both the formal curriculum and the life lessons of an important slice of the world that had been totally unknown to me, the "Rolodex in the sky" environment of influential men. I saw how the one-degree-of-separation world worked. We started with introductions. It was very jolly. Many around the table already knew each other, at least by reputation, and traded the years they graduated from the same Ivy League or prep schools or learned how their fraternity brother was related to someone else's wife. No public universities were represented in the room except by the two diversity fellows. It was a bit daunting.

I had two choices: to feel like an outclassed interloper or to try to use my Outsider's advantage. I came from a totally different background as a woman, a nurse, and a trade union official. I figured my experience must have been considered a plus for the group. That conclusion gave me the confidence to participate fully. And I was accepted as credible—because I had been vetted by the same people as everyone else there. It was really up to me to decide what happened after I took my seat.

Without a policy decision requiring affirmative outreach to find certain kinds of candidates, it is hard to imagine having such a tight leadership circle open up or be willing to accept me on an equal footing. For me, learning about the existence of this world and being a part of it, even for a few weeks, increased my self-assurance and opened many opportunities in the future. The final lesson from this story is that my presence opened doors for my classmates, too. Many quietly confided it was the first time they had interacted with a woman as an equal at the executive level.

Finding Top Women

A disconnect still exists between companies saying they are very interested in having women board members and recruiting practices that fail to look where the women who are ready to lead can be found. The Simmons School of Management, the nation's first business school designed for women, surveyed successful women managers and executives with an average of twenty years of work experience. It found that while close to half of these talented businesswomen had served on formal boards, only 11% were on for-profit ones; the rest were on nonprofit boards. Many women are gaining experience on nonprofit boards, but the search firms aren't looking where the candidates are.

Three practical recommendations can show corporate leaders a new direction if they are serious about diversity. First, ask, "Who don't we know?" instead of "Who do we know?" Change the search to include effective governance experience in nonprofits. Second, expand the qualification criteria to include successful entrepreneurial women. Last, have senior women executives network with their counterparts on smaller and/or nonprofit boards to locate qualified women.[3]

Other countries are exploring more expansive options to jump-start achieving balanced leadership by bringing more women to the corporate board table. These range from formal legislated quotas to more informal efforts by male top corporate executives.

Norway tried a voluntary approach in 2001, when the numbers of women directors were dismally low (about 6%). After two years about half of Norwegian companies still had no women on their boards, despite studies showing plenty of qualified women were ready to step up. With a history of well-accepted female elected leaders and near-equality in politics, the Norwegian government took a tougher approach: landmark legislation mandating that all publicly held companies have 40% women on their corporate boards within two years or face losing their corporate charters. This was a tough quota with even tougher sanctions.

This was not an antidiscrimination effort but a strategy to improve Norwegian business. It was the unlikely brainchild of a former businessman and Conservative minister for trade and industry, Ansgar Gabrielsen. His motivation was to get the best talent possible and end the practice of board members coming from "the same small circle of buddies who went hunting or fishing together." As he said, "The law was not about getting equality between the sexes; it was about the fact that diversity is a value in itself, that it creates wealth."[4]

Despite a hue and cry about not having enough qualified women, the draconian sanctions were not needed: the implied threat was enough. All but one corporation met the deadline, and now Norway has 40% women on corporate boards. Clearly, when Norway, Inc., really had to take a hard look, it found many, many talented women whom it had apparently been passing up.

The Professional Boards Forum established by Elin Hurvenes helped the companies in their search. I met Elin at the Salzburg Global Seminar, and she told us the secret to getting more women appointed when the atmosphere is strongly encouraging: "It is all about connections." Just as I had found at the Aspen Institute, having leaders get to know women as equals was part of the answer. It took her a year to develop the database of qualified and vetted women by looking beyond corporate management to the public sector, nonprofits, and entrepreneurs. She introduced those carefully chosen women to corporate board chairs and chief executives in a simulated boardroom challenge. So far, one thousand women have participated in her events, and half got board positions within the next year.

Other European countries are also exploring meaningful legislative standards to overcome long-standing inertia in the corporate world. Sweden set quotas and fines in 2006. Spain has set a six-year target to reach the 40% goal. Similar measures are under consideration in Finland and at the European level in the European Union.

In the United Kingdom, the Equal Opportunities Commission's "Sex and Power" report found women make up only 11% of directors in FTSE 100 companies (parallel to the U.S. Fortune 100). Serious discussions ensued about how to overcome the "pale male phenomenon." The United Kingdom has only 20% women in Parliament and had little appetite for legal quotas. However, outside pressure made new steps necessary. With other European countries moving quickly because of quotas, top British women were being attracted away. Something needed to be done.

FTSE is applying the Norwegian "connections" insight. In a one-on-one mentoring program led by Peninah Thomson, male executives of the FTSE 100 mentor competent, qualified senior women to prepare them for top corporate board positions beyond their own firms. The idea is being copied in Canada and France. The mentors are the ultimate Insiders, and the contacts and mentoring have resulted in more women moving up onto top boards.

The cross-firm, cross-industry mentoring approach is seen as a two-way street, not a favor to the women. The executive men learn more about "what it's like to be a woman in the corporate world" and how the behaviors of self-selecting male-dominated managerial groups make it difficult for "outsiders" to penetrate the circle and perform at their best. As one male executive said, "It can add to our long-term competitive advantage if we use diversity better than our competitors." For their part, the senior women build confidence and set career objectives. One mentor said, "A senior manager reaching out to a woman and saying, 'You're really good, you could be extremely successful' can be a very powerful intervention if it is well-targeted."[5]

In both Norway and the United Kingdom—with prodding and pressure from legislation or competition—top corporate executives moved to open the doors to the executive suite and bring more women to the table because it was smart business. In contrast, the United States is barely taking baby steps. Virtually no top male corporate leaders are engaged in increasing women's leadership opportunities. This remains framed as a "women's issue," with women essentially held responsible for breaking through.

International Measures to Bring More Women into Government

Politicians in many countries are learning the same lesson: It is good politics to bring more women into the halls of power. More than sixty widely varying countries in every corner of the world have a greater percentage of women in their national parliaments than the United States. This should be a wake-up call. Americans generally don't like to be behind the curve on progress.

Different countries with varying democratic political systems have gone about increasing women's representation in decision making in different ways. Can we learn from the countries that have formal targets or informal standards for women's representation? When leadership balance becomes an important priority, the results have been real partnerships between women and men making the big decisions for the future.

In some countries, political parties have made voluntary agreements to improve recruitment, training, and financial support for women candidates. The proportions of women elected have risen and fallen with the political fortunes of the various parties, particularly in those parliamentary democracies with national slates.[6] The United Kingdom is a case in point: the Labour Party landslide win in 1997 brought a large number of women into Parliament. As Labour's majority faded, so did the representation and power of women.

Constitutional change is the route taken in other countries, such as France, which has had parity (50:50 representation) since 1999. The catalyst for this change was a political manifesto published in 1996 by ten women from all the political parties. Countries writing new constitutions after civil wars, such as Rwanda and South Africa, have set out to foster true democracy and required significant proportions of women in their parliaments.

Takeaways

A lack of standards or benchmarks has left many women locked out of governance.

- Check your state legislature or city council.
- Check the board of your company or association.
- Check the policy about filling vacancies.

Use the levers you have to make "a woman in every pool" a reality.

Widen the net to fill a vacancy by asking, "Who do we need to know?"

Formal policies for balanced leadership can change the equation permanently.

Still other countries, such as India, have taken a legislative route. As discussed in Chapter 1, India has passed legislation requiring one-third of all village-level public offices to be held by women, and its Parliament is considering extending the concept to the national level. Women initially found it very difficult to be taken seriously in public life, but as their confidence and the evidence of their accomplishments grew, they received greater and greater acceptance. More women ran for office, more women won, and the 30% threshold has been not only reached but exceeded. On the ground, women officials brought big changes in priorities—clean water rather than roads, nurses and teachers rather than buildings. In India, as in South Africa, quota has been a floor, not a ceiling.

Gender Parity Efforts at Home

We can build on the very few existing gender parity approaches in the United States, which serve as precedents for the "women in every pool" strategy and get us at least a tiny bit closer to having a critical mass of women at power tables. Political parties have tried out some concepts in their party rules, a few legislative/gubernatorial initiatives have begun at the state level, and some dual Insider/Outsider strategies have been tried. Let's take political party efforts first, since involvement in party work often leads women to run for public office.

Both major political parties have formal policies on representation by women, and they are good case studies on how stronger standards can produce stronger results. The Republican Party has one woman, one man, and the party chair from each state on the national committee and "*endeavors* to have equal representation" in state delegations to the national convention. The Democratic Party has one man and one woman from each state on the national governing body and *requires* equal representation of convention delegates.

While they are only one factor, policies mandating, rather than simply encouraging, equal representation of women seem to have a positive effect on the proportion of women elected to office. Democratic women are being elected to Congress, statewide offices, and state legislatures two to three times as frequently as GOP women.[7]

Gender parity efforts have also popped up (mostly in the '80s and '90s) in some states—particularly Iowa, Pennsylvania, Oregon, Missouri, and New Jersey. Parity has generally been defined as at least 40% women in all appointed state offices, including as cabinet secretaries, agency heads, and commission and board members. Reviving and expanding upon these efforts will make a sizeable difference.

The Inside-Outside process generally starts with advocacy efforts by the women's community, then moves to either an executive order of the governor, a legislative resolution, or actual legislation requiring gender parity in appointments. Of these options, legislative action is most likely to cause lasting change. Meanwhile, women's organizations put together databases of well-qualified women who are interested in being appointed. While efforts have generally been at the state level, a parallel process could be used at local and city levels and for national boards and commissions.

A dual strategy is seeing some resurgence, and it is worth the effort, both moving elected officials to appoint more women and enabling women's groups to show how many women are ready to step up and lead. In Ohio, columnist Ann Fisher, writing in the *Columbus Dispatch*, analyzed the ap-

---

This Week I Will . . .

✔ Make sure conference programs I plan have strong women presenters and at least one-third women participants—even if I have to look for them myself.

✔ Share the "women in every pool" idea to update current practices and open opportunity for more women in my company and professional groups.

✔ Make the case with elected officials in my community about appointing more women to boards and commissions.

✔ Bring some women together to brainstorm how we can encourage women to send in their resumes for appointment.

---

pointments made by Governor Ted Strickland in his first eighteen months in office and found two out of three appointments went to men. The governor's office explained that only one-third of the applicants were women. Ann Fisher used her column to urge women to send in their resumes. Gubernatorial appointments are important: as Fisher put it, they not only "hold great cachet" but are a "resume-filler, an experience builder, a steppingstone to greater things, perhaps even public office."[8] The career ladder in political life includes being elected at some points and appointed at others.

Steppingstones where women gain experience, exposure, and expertise are too important to pass up. On the state level, appointments to commissions often open the door to other opportunities, since all are made through the governor's personnel office. Serving on a New York State health commission as a nurse and union official was very important to my job at the time but also turned out to be the entry point for later consideration as a top official in the Labor Department.

The proportion of women policy leaders in the executive branch of most state governments is rising ever so slowly (two-tenths of a percent total from 2001 to 2007).[9] It goes up when states have a woman governor or other statewide elected officials, then often drifts downward again unless the legislature has a strong women's caucus serving as a watchdog.

As in business, initial international studies are beginning to show a link between more women legislators and increased appointments of women. Political party standards make a big difference as well.

Momentum for Change: Practical Lessons

Five major developments give reason to hope our efforts will yield a wave of change:

- Domestic and international models—from "women in every pool" to benchmarks and standards—provide avenues to proceed.

- The evidence is on our side: balanced leadership positively affects the bottom line.

- We are in the right place at the right time, even if our skills are underutilized at the moment; a competition for talent at home and globally matches our high education levels and styles of leadership.

- Times are changing, with younger generations of Americans sold on diversity as strength and articulating goals for life balance previously seen only in women's publications.

- The glass ceiling has cracked, even if it hasn't shattered, and at least a few women have moved up almost everywhere.

Women are in positions of authority now—in business, politics, and the community. We have both a platform and a shared agenda for action. Each of us, with supportive men as partners, can be part of making a new reality if we take responsibility to wedge the door open for more women. You can use the "women in every pool" strategy and work for policies that will yield more women in influential places in companies, organizations, and communities. You can challenge elected officials to be accountable and provide the resumes of qualified women candidates to appoint. Changing the ground rules and creating new standards means more and more women will lead the way.

10 Together, We Rise

The final tool, networking, brings together all of the steps on your journey to leadership and the 30% Solution. Networking will build our strength more quickly and easily, expedite changing the ground rules, support you as a transformational leader, and set the stage for the world we want to see. As you build your network, reach out, and connect, we will all rise.

Historically, women in the United States have been transformational leaders, change agents to move society forward. Our foremothers were abolitionists, founders of settlement houses, organizers of winning efforts to end child labor and establish a forty-hour week, suffragettes, and fighters for equality. Now you can be part of advocacy networks to achieve paid sick leave and expanded family leave policies, close the gender wage gap, and clear the way for more women decision makers. By linking people, you can create a better future.

As you move forward, remember: relationships are primary; all else is secondary. I heard this advice first at a conference from Dr. Ron David, a pediatrician, chaplain, and former university professor. It is critical to building a top-performing team or bringing unlikely allies together to accomplish a goal. Coalitions that come together because of a single common interest (with or without shared long-range goals) are actually best

Test the Strength of Your Networks

- Do you have a mentor and/or a trusted circle of advisors? Do you keep in touch? Are you also available to help them?

- Do you have a network of other professionals to draw on to solve problems?

- Are you part of your alumni group or professional association?

- Do you participate in a women's network or community organization?

- Are you part of social networks like Plaxo, LinkedIn, MySpace, and/or Facebook? Is your information up to date?

- Are you engaged in online advocacy efforts to change from what is to what should be?

held together by personal relationships, not organizational titles or the overarching objectives of the work.

How Are Your Personal Networks?

Women are great at forming relationships, and networks are just webs of relationships and connections. Many women are strong at forming linkages with family, neighbors, and friends, but don't bring that strength into their business or political life, or even realize how important it is. The quiz in the box above will get you thinking about consciously building stronger networks for yourself.

The press has carried stories about a backlash against the term "networking" as connoting a formal, one-way, false, or calculating relationship.[1] Like anything else, networking can be misused or taken to extremes. Our focus here is on two-way, genuine, and mutually beneficial networking that is often informal. Actually, informal networks are the primary ones to help you build your own career and wedge the door open. It doesn't make sense to ignore their potential benefits: inspiration, information, contacts, mentors, support, and encouragement.

In many ways these networks are your secret to success, helping you feel connected instead of isolated, burned out, or bummed out. As the McKinsey Leadership Project puts it, "People with strong networks and good mentors enjoy more promotions, higher pay, and greater career satisfaction. They feel a sense of belonging, which makes their lives meaningful."[2]

My own networks gave me invaluable advice and support as I worked on this book. Friends, family, and professional colleagues generously helped me find resources, set up interviews, implement focus groups, and identify cutting-edge research. They reviewed drafts and even participated in surveys to find the very best title for the book. They gave me broad input and connections to the work of other women and men who care about why women's leadership matters. The original circle has continued to widen into a community of interest as people in my networks have introduced me to their contacts.

Do you have a mutual support network of coworkers and friends to share ideas, pat you on the back, cheer you on, or give you real or virtual hugs when times are tough? My mother used to call this a "mutual admiration society." Whom can you call on to help you solve a difficult problem? Are you still in touch with people you mentored and special former colleagues? If you have a small business, do you have a network of suppliers and customers or clients that can be expanded?

Do you have a network of friends—women and men—from the neighborhood, college buddies, or professional colleagues you can count on, learn from, and connect through? Does your town have a women's network? Are you part of the virtual networks working to remove unnecessary hurdles to women's advancement?

Be resolute in looking at your own networks, updating and improving them for greater career and personal satisfaction. Reserve some of your time to stay in contact and be available to help others. The rewards are stronger relationships, more information, new friends and colleagues, the excitement of engaging with others, and the potential to partner together for fun or progress.

A look at your e-mail in-box will give you one clue to the state of your current networks. The formal ones with Listservs are easiest to spot.

Allison Fine has written that "the Connected Age is a boon for women" since we have the innate ability to connect, share information, and collaborate, and the medium allows us to write, blog, or answer on our own time. E-mail is a leveler for busy lives and is a neutral environment where your gender and looks are largely irrelevant.[3] If you need some help to get up to speed, ask what Fine calls "a NetGenner" to mentor you. People born after 1975 or so have a seemingly effortless ability to use personal computers, wireless e-mails, texting, and cell phones to network.

Social networking sites are newer tools for staying in touch. Checking out who is—and is not—on your lists is worth your time. You might discover that responding to requests from others to include you in their networks has made your own more haphazard than you would like. In contrast, you might be or become the glue or hub holding a network or even a network of networks together. This is a much better option, making it more likely you will be able to count on getting the personal and professional resources you need and be seen as a valuable resource to others.

More broadly, whether your initial network is a virtual one, an informal lunch group, a community group, or a formal caucus or committee, it is worth thinking about all the others and how to link them together. Each one offers ways to form relationships; trade information about possible job openings, professional services, or markets; share ideas to solve problems; provide gravitas for women's ideas; and add spice to your work.

The Power of Virtual Networks

Networks, especially virtual ones, can have incredible reach. For example, the Salzburg Power Network is a group of women and a few men who have been fellows at the Salzburg Global Seminars on breaking the glass ceiling in business and politics. The network spans the globe and provides ongoing insights and fresh ideas to bring back home. Two of the most inspiring for me involved women's networks in Ghana and Kuwait.

One of the Salzburg network members, businesswoman and parliamentarian Hanna Tetteh-Kpodar, is now the minister for trade, industry and private sector development in Ghana. The platform of her party includes a women's manifesto created through a broad-based process involving women's groups, nongovernmental organizations, locally elected women across the country, media women and men, and representatives of all political parties. The manifesto raises issues of concern, including underrepresentation of women in decision making, and sets forth a set of demands to address them. Its adoption by the party empowered women to use their votes as a bargaining tool. We could take some lessons.

At a Salzburg seminar I also learned how women in Kuwait finally got the right to vote—under the radar and out of the eye of the press—by using new technology. Kuwait is a very conservative Muslim country where religious tradition calls for women to wear an *abaya*, a full-length black overgarment covering everything except the face, feet, and hands, when they are out in public. It was the last nation in the world to enfranchise women. We can learn from the women in that society how to network for change here at home. Kuwait's emir, Sheikh Jaber al Ahmed al Sabah, issued a decree to enfranchise women in 1999, but the Parliament blocked it. Rola Dashti led a networking campaign to obtain parliamentary backing for the decree. The campaigners won that backing in 2005 by seeming to be everywhere. They arranged instantaneous meet-up rallies via cell phone, and they sent widely disseminated text messages and blast faxes to followers and the press, holding male leaders accountable for their pro forma rhetoric about equality with a campaign to "bring Kuwait into the 21st century." In the 2006 election, women voters outnumbered men.[4] In 2009, four women, including Rola, were elected to the Parliament (8% of its members).[5]

The same electronic organizing strategies were used successfully by MoveOn.org and then the Obama campaign to get out the vote in 2008. In the women's community, MomsRising, led by Joan Blades (also a founder of MoveOn.org), is using electronic networks to mobilize moms—both in the workforce and at home—to take action around a common agenda, including fair pay, child care, maternity and paternity leave, and open, flexible work.

One of the most impressive results of the Beijing conference on women has been the growth of networks connecting women from the global South (generally developing countries) and North (generally industrialized countries) to learn from each other and share policies, strategies, wins, and losses. The networks are two-way streets. For example, microenterprise lending began with the Grameen Bank in Bangladesh. The concept was essentially unknown in the United States prior to the conference. Microenterprise investment has grown rapidly now that the accomplishments of enterprising women creating businesses and paying back their loans have become known, largely through personal networking relationships and virtual women's networks. Now financing programs exist in the United States and through the World Bank and United Nations Development Fund to invest in this powerful strategy, which lifts families out of poverty through the achievements of women.

Women's Networks Bring Community Change

Networks of women working in the community can have powerful cumulative effects. Often, as momentum builds, newer and larger changes happen as a result of these strong personal relationships.

In Chicago, for example, women leaders from business, politics, philanthropy, and nonprofits got to know each other through an informal network that started the Chicago Foundation for Women. As the circle widened they worked together in various capacities for women's advancement and community betterment over a number of years. One participant started the discussion this way: "Everyone in this room has made a difference and has a story." Their successes were on tough community problems not traditionally considered "women's issues," such as the need for reform of the juvenile justice system. These leaders used their informal networks to solve these problems, bringing "distinctive energy and collaborative style to the work" and drawing strength from the accomplishments of other women. At a focus group, one of these leaders noted, "We seem to be talking through the lens of a 'female strategy,' with the compassion or courage to fight for what's right." Lots of heads nodded. Would the changes have happened without women leading the way? The answer was, "Not likely."[6]

Similarly, a network of Denver women leaders in philanthropy first worked together to create the Women's Foundation of Colorado, spearheaded by a visionary leader, Ambassador Swanee Hunt.[7] The ripples of this women's network have influenced change ever more widely through the community by leading change in mainstream and larger foundations.[8]

Stories of success are seldom told unless we take time within our own personal networks to take stock of our collective positive impact. A Chicago focus group of women in finance raised this point. One participant, the former chief investment officer of a large religious organization and mother of a thirty-something daughter, said, "We've made a big difference, but the stories have not been passed down." In addition to being high flyers in business, many of these women were networked through their deep involvement in religious and spiritual work. They began to talk about how to pass down the stories to help women be more comfortable being visionary and bring their spirituality and desire to "make a difference" holistically into leadership. The head of entrepreneurship for a university business school articulated the potential of transformative change "if women, working in the 'white space,' could bring women's values of giving back into the whole society."[9]

Building a Community Women's Network

Would you enjoy and benefit from a breakfast, lunch, or tea group—a network by another name—of women in similar positions to yours in different companies or organizations? Some of the best advice I got about running a nonprofit came from a breakfast group of women CEOs of other organizations of various types and sizes. We met for several years. When I needed to do a salary survey, someone in the group had already done one and had ideas about how to proceed. When another CEO had a really big problem with her trustees, we could talk over possible courses of action and be a sounding board for her. The approach was simple. We took turns arranging the location and sending out notices for the first Tuesday of the month. Each of us could introduce another woman into the group. Everyone paid for her own meal (often a bagel in a conference room). Everything we discussed was confidential. It worked well.

How about you? Could you find the time for one lunch a month to share experiences with other women on your contact list? How about having each woman bring one friend the next time? Soon you will have many more contacts and friendships among the career women in your hometown. Job vacancies and educational opportunities are likely to surface. Women you don't know yet could be ideal candidates for a position your firm is trying to fill, or you might hear about a great job for yourself. Speakers can provide ideas and information to widen your horizon. And you'll have a deep source of contacts to tap when you are faced with a difficult situation.

Women Leading Kentucky (WLK) grew just this way. Janet Holloway, one of the founders and now executive director, has shepherded the growth of this professional nonprofit network of women and men committed to helping women lead and learn. Its programs are designed to develop relationships based on respect and mutual support among people who share the goal of creating business and leadership opportunities for women. Its motto, "Some leaders are born women," and message, "If I can do it, so can you," have led to connections among over two thousand women leaders in Lexington, enhanced their businesses, improved the business climate for women, and promoted a vision of a city where women achieve in every sector.[10]

WLK's regular monthly roundtable networking luncheons draw a hundred or more women and a few men to hear a guest speaker, and there is a larger annual event. When I spoke there, the audience included women from the university, the police department, local government, health institutions, business (small and large) and finance, nonprofits, the media, and sponsoring organizations. The atmosphere was electric, and business cards were flying.

Nine of the women who currently lead this dynamic network met with me as an informal focus group. They spanned diverse generations, races, backgrounds, and sectors. They pointed out that in Kentucky, new female state legislators are given terrible offices in the basement to "show

Giant Oaks from Little Acorns Grow

Tiny networks can grow into powerful forces. Emily's List is a dynamic network of women and men who are committed to seeing more pro-choice Democratic women in top political offices—and are putting their money behind it.

Ellen Malcolm, the founder and president, describes the beginnings this way: She got a group of eight friends together one night. Each woman brought her contact lists, and they sat together and wrote to ask friends to join this new network, which was raising money for women to run for political office and win.

One of the largest and most effective political action committees in the country grew from this dinner party. The "Emily" in Emily's List stands for Early Money Is Like Yeast. Many women in Congress owe a great deal of their support in winning elections to Emily—and her friends.

them," and some women are still "culturally controlled by their husbands, who tell them not only what to do but also how to vote." WLK helps overcome low self-confidence and helps women who do get to the top to deliver on what other women need. These leaders believe strongly that showing the strength of women sharing with women—networking, supporting, encouraging, and mentoring—will empower women to see their own leadership potential.[11]

If you'd like to join an existing network but your community doesn't have anything like WLK, no doubt you can find chapters of membership organizations, including women's, professional, religious, activist, and businesswomen's groups, where you can connect up with others interested in opening doors for women. Numerous cities, counties, states, and universities have commissions on the status of women, women's lobbies, or women's agenda groups with programs and activities for advancing women. Increasingly, organizations like Rotary International and local chambers of commerce are welcoming businesswomen into their ranks.

In politics, women's networks can be especially powerful if they can use an Inside-Outside strategy. A good case in point was a breakthrough on an issue affecting millions of American women: a requirement for insurance carriers to cover contraceptives if they covered other prescription drugs. Advocates had worked forever state by state to win insurance coverage of contraceptives as a major health and wellness issue and a significant cost item for women of childbearing age. A women legislators' network was outraged that contraceptives were still not covered. When Viagra was covered as soon as it came on the market, they seized the moment. As Democratic State Senator Jackie Speier, a sponsor of the legislation in California, noted, the coverage of Viagra made arguments against mandated contraceptive coverage "laughable, really. No one can argue it with a straight face anymore."[12]

Putting together an Inside-Outside strategy with advocates, the network simultaneously introduced legislation in thirty states. Seven of these passed bills the first year (Connecticut, Georgia, Hawaii, Maine, Nevada, New Hampshire, and North Carolina), with many more following suit later. This burst of activity didn't just happen. It was a striking example of the potential power of women's leadership networks and women working together across state lines and parties to achieve the common goal of decreasing unintended pregnancies.[13]

Investing Time in Advocacy Networks to Make It Easier for Women to Lead

Advocacy networks are another arena where you can build your skills, confidence, and contacts. As we discussed earlier, outdated business practices still limit women's options and are very costly to society. No matter how talented you are or how much experience and education you have, it will be rougher for you and other women to step up as leaders if the old customs of the workplace stay in place. They were created for a different world and are no longer relevant. They will remain the same, however, without policy change, which provides the structure and standards to go from the familiar to the new and more effective. If you want to be part of the solution, get involved in an advocacy network or organization. Such networks are an integral component in the Inside-Outside strategy we have been exploring. Electronic advocacy networks are in place, and you can easily connect to them with the click of a mouse. Participation, usually at no cost unless you choose to donate to support the effort, widens your worldview, increases your knowledge of possible solutions, and broadens your own contacts, as well as building support for change.

Earlier we talked about ways for you to help bring about flexible work arrangements and grow the women's business sector through contracting. Advocacy networks work on these issues, too, as detailed in the Resources section. Other concerns vital to women—including child care and early education, access to health care through universal health insurance coverage, and portability of retirement savings—are on the national agenda, thanks in large part to the work of such groups.

Further policies necessary to equalize opportunities for women to move up include provision of paid sick leave and family leave and pay equity. These concerns of working families require women's leadership specifically because women understand their importance and see them as priorities. Through advocacy networks working on these issues, you can join with others who share your desire for a world where it is as easy for women as for men to rise to the level of our talents, skills, and interests. Let's discuss these issues, and these networks, in a little more detail.

Paid Sick Leave and Family Leave

Many women feel like they are walking on a tightrope. There is no safety net of benefits to provide income if they are ill, have or adopt a baby, or need to handle family health emergencies.

In the United States, far too many working families are not covered by paid sick leave or parental leave. Employers choose whether or not to provide these as benefits rather than sharing responsibility in case of illness, pregnancy, adoption, or family emergency. The absence of paid sick leave and paid family leave lowers both productivity and family well-being.

Approximately one-half of all American full-time workers in the private sector do not have paid sick leave.[14] The only jurisdictions that require employers to provide a certain number of paid sick days are Washington,

D.C., San Francisco, and Milwaukee. If you live anywhere else, are an hourly or contract worker, work for a company that doesn't provide this benefit, and get sick, you face difficult options. You can work anyway, or lose family income and possibly your job. We hear a lot about the costs of absenteeism, but some studies now show the costs of "presenteeism" (where you come to work and share your germs and/or are minimally productive) may actually be greater.[15]

A similar portion of American workers are eligible for twelve weeks of unpaid family and medical leave under federal law because they work for companies with more than fifty employees and have been on the job for a year. Many mothers and fathers can't afford to take the time off, though, especially when family expenses are likely to increase.

President Obama campaigned on a platform of passing both paid sick leave and family leave legislation, and action is expected. However, tough opposition will make passage difficult. You can make a difference by linking up with others in an effective advocacy network. Start at the top-notch campaign website of the National Partnership for Women and Families, where you can get information and sign up to be part of the action on campaigns in twelve states and Congress. Recent national action on paid family leave has focused on federal employees and military families. California, New Jersey, and Washington State now have paid leave for all their residents, though the details of the coverage vary considerably, and coalition efforts were under way in 2008 in Arizona, Massachusetts, Minnesota, New York, and Pennsylvania.

The Gender Wage Gap

The gender wage gap is an unseen factor underlying the stress career women feel. No matter how hard you work or how much education you get, the gap is omnipresent and saps the incomes of millions of dual-earner couples and single women, especially single moms. The median income for women who work full time, full year is $31,900 (half of all working women make less). The comparable male figure includes a 24% premium: an additional $7,800 per year. According to the National Women's Law Center, if work-

---

This Week I Will . . .

✔ Take the first step in building a lasting mentoring relationship with one person I respect who has more experience than I have to give me new ideas and extend my personal support network.

✔ Check to see if my community has a women's network where I could meet new people and broaden my own network.

✔ Sign up for a social network and/or bring my profile up to date and add my personal contacts.

✔ Do my share to make change happen by becoming part of an advocacy network on an issue I want to see resolved, such as paid leave or equal pay.

---

ing women earned the same as men who work the same number of hours; have the same education, age, and union status; and live in the same region of the country, their annual family incomes would rise by $4,000, and the poverty rate would be cut in half.[16]

Whichever way you look at it, women get the short end of the wage stick. The gap grows after age thirty and is even greater for African American and Hispanic women. Two-thirds of all adults earning minimum wage are women. A minimum-wage worker must put in a virtually impossible seventy-two hours a week, fifty-two weeks a year, to get to the poverty level of $19,000 for a family of four. And lower wages lead to a significant deficit in retirement income for women's later years.

The Supreme Court's five-to-four decision in *Ledbetter v. Goodyear* in 2007 was a setback to efforts to close the wage gap. Lilly M. Ledbetter worked for nineteen years as a manager at a Goodyear plant. In 1997 she learned she was earning less than the lowest-paid man in the department. She immediately sued her employer, but the high court ruled she had waited too long after originally suffering discrimination. It was a classic catch-22 situation: after nearly twenty years of being paid less than the men who worked for her, she had no recourse because she had not known about the discrimination.[17]

The Lilly Ledbetter Act overturning the Supreme Court ruling was the first piece of legislation signed by President Obama. The clock on bringing such discrimination cases now begins to run when someone learns she is being unfairly and illegally treated. Closing this loophole was an important step, but there is much left to do to close the pay gap.

You can make a difference by joining a national network or organization working to achieve equal pay. The Pay Equity Campaign leads an educational effort to increase understanding about ways to close the gap and sponsors Equal Pay Day. The National Women's Law Center's Fair Pay Campaign is advocating passage of the Paycheck Fairness Act. Again, with the new administration, the possibility of change is in the air, but it won't happen without strong advocacy networks of women and men who see the impact on family budgets and work together to overcome inertia and press for positive action.

· · ·

Together, we rise. Your networks will both bring you support and help you make the way up easier for the women who come behind you.

We have one more frontier to cross. What do we want the world to look like when women take our places at the power tables? Having a vision is essential. The Conclusion leads us to dream bigger dreams for a better future.

Conclusion
Dreaming Bigger Dreams

Get out your crystal ball. Where do you think we should be in 2020, one hundred years after women won the right to vote? When (not if) the leadership gap is closed, the power and potential of women will be freed up so we can bring forward our values, passion, and intellect. Our career and caring contributions will be valued and respected and our voices heard clearly, not muted or filtered. By taking our seats at decision-making tables on a more equal basis, we are challenged to make a difference. It's time to act on our dreams, building on today's women-centered initiatives to change the world.

An inexorable wave of change—really a revolution—has ended eons of male determinism in the home, the family, the economy, and political life. This revolution has made your life different from those of women in the generations before you.

We are standing on the shoulders of the courageous women and men at the Seneca Falls Convention in 1848. They called for a two-word amendment to the Declaration of Independence: "We hold these truths to be self-evident; that all men *and women* are created equal . . ."[1]

The right to vote was finally achieved seventy-two years later, in 1920—such a short time ago that my mother was born before then. It was less than forty years ago that women achieved equal protection under the law in terms of employment, education, sports, credit, pregnancy, and property rights. That isn't so long ago either: In the early '70s, I qualified for a mortgage based on my income but was required by law to have a male cosigner.

We have made great progress, but there is still much work ahead of us. The Constitution does not include an Equal Rights Amendment. African American women, Latinas, immigrant women, all find the upward path much more difficult. And women's leadership remains incidental in our major institutions; in business, government, universities, religious institutions, and professions, the top tier is, at best, "tokenism plus a few."

By 2020, one hundred years after women's suffrage, we should see another sea change. We should have surpassed the 30% Solution and be reaching parity; policies as if women mattered should be considered usual, not exceptional.

What will be different when women are fully empowered? See how your ideas match this picture: "Women's empowerment will be achieved when the human rights of women and men are equally recognized under law, and women have respect, responsibility and opportunity, power and voice in their personal lives, families and communities, the economy and the body politic which are neither diminished nor stereotyped because of gender."[2]

The political, economic, legal, and cultural advancement of women moves along a five-stage continuum (see box). Across the world the historical, cultural, and legal shifts have moved back and forth along the same pattern but at different rates of change, influenced by racial, ethnic, economic, geographic, religious, and age dimensions.[3] But the final stage is always women and men as equal partners in deciding the future.

When enough women like you step into leadership roles, we will reach that stage of partnership, and our voices will be heard. What will we say? Will we be thinking big enough to make the kinds of changes we often dream about?

Old Problems, New Perspectives

Let's look at the big picture of how full empowerment of women is important not only for women, families, and individual companies and organi-

---

The Women's Empowerment Continuum

Women as property of their husbands/fathers without any individual rights

Women as separate persons but unequal under law

Women as victims of discrimination and seeking redress

Women and men as equals in all spheres

Women and men as partners to create a shared vision for the future

---

zations, but for economic prosperity and social welfare. Gender inequality is the common denominator of big, apparently intractable problems such as poverty, violence, risks to families, and the disconnect between further education and better salaries. With more women at the helm we can—and must—move further and faster to forge solutions.

The face of poverty is women and children. Women are widely discussed as the key to healthy development of poor countries, but much more needs to be done around the globe and here at home. Two-thirds of the world's poor are women and children, and two-thirds of adults who are illiterate are women. Antipoverty strategies in this country fail to utilize proven women's self-sufficiency approaches to move families out of poverty. Instead, the proportion of American children in poverty is climbing.

Violence is a scourge affecting one out of three women and girls everywhere in the world. Issues sometimes seen as separate—child abuse by loved ones; sexual harassment on the job; domestic violence in the home; rape and sexual assault on the streets or even on dates; and rape, pregnancy, and sexual abuse as weapons of war—all involve power figures (generally men) attacking the less powerful (women and children) because they feel it is "their right" and they can do so with impunity.

Working families face unnecessarily high risks. In the United States, in contrast to other industrialized countries, high-quality and affordable early care and education for young children is not widely available, and even less support exists for care for elderly family members. Many, many families are without adequate health care—even those with insurance. As discussed earlier, no standards exist for sick leave, and almost half of all full-time workers have none. Family leave is not available to everyone and does not replace income, so many parents are virtually required to return to work even with newborns at home.

Education is not consistently linked with higher earning power. The "American dream" holds that increased education will result in higher earnings, but that is an unfulfilled promise for millions of American women. Women college graduates make less than three-quarters of what men earn, and earnings for professional women in every field lag behind educational attainment.

In addition, the market undervalues caring for human beings in occupations largely held by women (nursing, teaching, early education, elder care), and those who perform these jobs consistently receive low wages regardless of their education level. It is useful to compare the entry-level salaries of a few different occupations for holders of a bachelor's degree. A fairly dramatic shortage of nurses in many parts of the country and unionization of nurses have increased salaries for many nurses, who have an average starting salary of $45,191, compared to a software developer, who begins at $59,806.[4] Salaries for other professionals, such as early childhood and kindergarten teachers, continue to be consistently too low at $32,000 to attract and retain top talent despite extensive longitudinal research demonstrating their value to society as well as the children.[5]

As full partners with the authority and responsibility to lead and create new answers in business, politics, and the community, will we think and act boldly to catalyze transformation? Can we creatively attack these old problems and go further?

Build on Experience

On the international stage, women-centered models are being tested on a large scale. Women's innovations, research, leadership, and advocacy

Are We Thinking Big Enough?

The *Economist*, a well-regarded international business publication, editorialized in April 2006, "Forget India, China and the internet: economic growth is driven by women."

Can we unapologetically bring this vision home to America?

have paved the way—and the mostly male leaders of countries and multinational corporations have determined that women's advancement is the most effective way to go. Women's advancement is becoming an accepted cornerstone to build economies and democracies. Women-led initiatives in the United States have also been tested and show promise. With balanced leadership, women can be partners in implementing change on a much wider scale. Take a look at the examples below.

Invest seriously in women to yield economic dividends. The World Bank is working to build the economies of developing countries by using women-centered programs as a primary focus. The World Bank Action Plan, titled "Gender Equality as Smart Economics," is based on the proven thesis that restricting economic opportunity for women is bad economic policy. The plan resulted from extensive consultations and was ratified unanimously as a major investment goal by the finance ministers of countries around the world. I met with Amanda Ellis, World Bank senior gender advisor, to learn more.[6]

Over the next few years, the action plan will continue to be implemented in four areas, with various key partners using clear performance indicators and metrics to test its success in a series of developing countries. The entire World Bank Group is committed to a major sustained investment in these four areas: using a gender lens to understand the problem; providing special initiatives to empower women; collecting strong data and performing comprehensive evaluations; and sharing the lessons learned. As one of the first steps, $100 million has been committed in commercial credit lines to women entrepreneurs.

The corporate sector, which has invested charitable dollars in women's advancement initiatives, is now starting to take an exciting business investment approach as well. Goldman Sachs has launched a "10,000 Women Initiative," a $100 million, five-year global program to provide business and management education to ten thousand underserved women, primarily in developing countries. It projects that narrowing the gender gap in employment will increase per capita income up to 14% worldwide by 2020 compared with baseline projections.[7] A number of academic partners are expanding the reach of this effort. For example, the Yale School of Public Health is partnering with Tsinghua University to provide management and leadership education to Chinese women working in public health.[8]

Our challenge is to build on the World Bank and Goldman Sachs experience. Investment in women is needed, particularly in economically deprived areas of the United States (including rural areas and center cities) and in underserved groups (including minority and immigrant women as well as those with disabilities). It should include business and management education and access to capital resources, technical assistance, and peer support.

Some very promising domestic initiatives in this area actually preceded international agreement on the centrality of women to moving families out of poverty. They have shown excellent results but have had difficulties sustaining their funding base. Many policy makers have a blind spot when it comes to women and poverty and are still in a charity mode. Sara Gould, president of the Ms. Foundation, summarized it this way: "Women and economic development are never in the same sentence. They are seen as an oxymoron."[9]

Women's foundations have led the way, but it hasn't been easy. The Ms. Foundation, best known for "Take Our Daughters and Sons to Work," began holding institutes for grassroots leaders fighting poverty through a women-centered approach twenty years ago. In 1991 it spearheaded a Collaborative Fund for Women's Economic Development. Through a competitive grant process, individuals and foundations developed or expanded local programs based on women's self-sufficiency. The results have been impressive: thirty-four groups have been funded, and thousands of women have brought themselves up by their bootstraps—with help and support. However, with each succeeding round it has been more difficult to sustain the level of investment, since many funding partners move on to new priorities every three years.

The Stepping Stones project, which is "paving women's pathways to economic security," was launched after the Washington Area Women's Foundation released its profile of women and girls in the Washington, D.C., area (see Chapter 7). This program builds the long-term financial independence and economic security of local low-income, women-headed families. It has developed partnerships with one hundred community groups, foundations, and corporations, and with the local and federal governments. One of the program's four components, the Financial Education and Wealth Creation Fund (supported by private donors, philanthropic and corporate foundations, and a special federal appropriation to the D.C. government), in two years of operation has increased the assets of 296 women a total of $3.5 million and helped them accumulate an additional $2.5 million in home equity by reducing debt, increasing savings, and refinancing homes. Anne Mosle, then president of the foundation, tells about a woman in the program who said, "Everything I've been able to do, I was helped by a woman. Now I have my back covered when I take a risk."[10] Again, finding the resources to continue and expand this excellent project is the biggest challenge.

Clearly, serious investment in women can create economic growth and support families to get on their feet. What domestic investor—private or governmental—will take the lead here to do what the World Bank and Goldman Sachs are doing on a global scale? Who can make that happen? Are you in a position to press for consideration of this strategy in your company or community?

Advance and empower women as a competitiveness strategy. The World Economic Forum (WEF), under the leadership of Laura Tyson, a prominent American economist, and Saadia Zahidi, WEF associate director, began doing an annual Gender Gap Index in 2002 as a "framework for quantifying the magnitude of gender-based disparities and designing effective measures to reduce them . . . and optimize the use of talent." WEF founder and executive chairman Klaus Schwab has explained why this group, the ultimate Insiders organization, would undertake such an effort. Its annual Davos conferences are attended by powerful leaders of countries, the financial world, corporations, and universities, and are covered endlessly by the business pages. It is a rather unlikely cheerleader for countries and companies to close the gender gap.

Schwab explains that "one of the fundamental cornerstones of economic growth available to them [countries and companies] is the skills and talents of the human resources pool. Women not only make up one half of this potential talent base, they also contribute to bringing in some different perspectives that are so important in a complex, inter-dependent and fast-moving world."[11] The index measures how much men and women in each country differ on four measures—education, health, economic participation, and political participation—and uses the size of the gap between them to rank countries. The United States ranks well down the list, pulled down by the pay gap and dismal statistics about women in political decision making.[12] Policy makers in other parts of the world watch this report closely as they assess how to be as competitive as possible.

Now that you know why a prestigious international economic organization is investing so much in measures of women's advancement, you might ask whether it is taking action on its findings—and why there isn't a comparable group in the United States with a similar focus. WEF has established a Global Gender Parity Group made up of 50% women and 50% men from business, politics, academia, and the media to work together to develop "creative and visible strategies to optimize the use of talent." U.S. executives, particularly from the federal government and multinational corporations, participate every year at Davos. Why have they not taken up the WEF's premise that closing the leadership gender gap is essential to improve U.S. competitiveness in the global marketplace?

It isn't easy to see the whole picture here on how women are faring as critical economic players. As the saying goes, "We measure what we value and value what we measure." The United States simply doesn't measure. No comparable credible business or governmental entity does similar benchmarking of progress across the states. Women's research organizations have worked hard to fill the gap,[13] but "Outsider" data have less impact than a decision by an Insider or neutral agency or business group that women's advancement is critical to competitiveness and worth measuring and monitoring.

Our challenge is to build on the WEF's competitiveness strategy. State-by-state comparisons in this country would be as powerful as the WEF's data comparing countries and could spur significant progress as states competed to improve their records and permitted monitoring. The U.S. Census Bureau or another government agency could be charged with this responsibility. Alternatively, a major business group could provide the rankings. Two logical candidates are the Committee for Economic Development (made up of CEOs from business and academia) and the Business Roundtable (two hundred or so top business leaders). Both have only a sprinkling of women on their boards. National organizations of state governors or legislators that could take this up have a similar composition. However, women Insiders could work with advocates Outside and make change happen.

Equalize resource allocation using a gender lens. The United Nations Development Fund for Women (UNIFEM) is helping countries use gender budgeting to distribute precious public resources, including capital, education, and health care, more equitably to bring about change. Australia inaugurated gender budgeting in the mid-'80s, followed by South Africa and the Philippines. Currently twenty-two countries are looking at where men and women's needs are the same and where they are different and allocating resources accordingly for the greatest impact. Most recently, the finance ministers of Nepal, Morocco, and Egypt have begun implementing such programs.

This concept is still pretty much unknown in the United States—except in San Francisco, which adopted the Convention on the Elimination of

All Forms of Discrimination against Women (CEDAW, or the Women's Treaty) in 1998 as the basis for women's legal rights in the city. San Francisco then began to assess the differential impacts of governmental policies on women and men (broken down by race, immigrant and parental status, education, age, disability, etc.). By 2008, new resources were being made available to meet unmet needs such as sexual abuse counseling of girls in the juvenile justice system, flexible work schedules citywide, and improved street lighting in poorly lit areas. Many more women were also being appointed to boards and commissions.[14]

Our challenge is to build on UNIFEM's gender budgeting experience. Every municipality, city, county, and state, as well as the federal government, has the potential to put gender budgeting into place on a voluntary basis or by legislation or executive action. Tax dollars should be invested where they will have the greatest impact, so gender budgeting is smart budgeting, not a handout for a special interest group. Women elected officials and/or women's commissions could take the lead. Women's foundations and funds, many of which have done reports on the status of women in their jurisdiction, or statewide women's agenda or women's lobby groups could become the Outside catalysts to see that gender budgeting becomes a reality.

Cover womenomics as a mainstream business issue. The *Economist*, an international weekly business publication read by influential business leaders and public policy makers, has drawn attention to the importance of women to economic growth and viability. In April 2006 it coined the phrase "womenomics" to crystallize the importance of women in the economy. It headlined its special report, "The future of the world economy lies increasingly in female hands."[15]

The editors have returned again and again to this topic in an interesting attempt to educate top decision makers on how a change in current thinking is in their best interests. Taking the position that "if more women were in paid work, the world could be much richer,"[16] they have explained how sex discrimination in employment and education in Asia costs up to $77 billion per year and highlighted a report showing that the United States' GDP would be up to 9% higher —an enormous boost—if employment rates were equalized. Before the latest financial crisis, the *Economist* published "Womenomics Revisited," which stated, "Men run the world's economies; but it may be up to women to rescue them." Unfortunately, it doesn't seem that policy makers were listening.

In contrast, domestic media seldom venture beyond reports on "first women" and general personal-interest stories on women in top political or economic jobs—often focused on how they balance their family responsibilities.

Our challenge is to build on the coverage model of the Economist. Regional publications (e.g., *Crain's Business*), mainstream weekly and monthly business magazines (e.g., *Business Week, Forbes, Fast & Company*), and the *Wall Street Journal* and other national newspapers with a well-read business beat should accept the challenge to educate American business leaders about the untapped potential of women to grow their businesses and the economy.

Implementing U.S. versions of what we have learned from the international experience will make a big difference by 2020. Serious investment in women's self-sufficiency pays economic dividends for families and society. Advancing and empowering women is a smart competitiveness strategy for a company and the country. Equalizing the use of tax dollars by using gender analysis and budgeting means greater impact. Womenomics is in the best interest of business and should be seen and publicized as a mainstream business strategy. There is still an uphill climb to bring these exciting concepts home to America, but it will happen with more women transformative leaders at the helm.

Five Big Dreams for 2020

What else will be different in 2020 in this country with balanced leadership? Let's dream five big dreams and, just as in the fairy tales, make them come true.

Takeaways

- International success stories on the benefits of women's advancement give us a new frame of reference and challenge us to do better.

- As leaders we can promote answers: self-sufficiency instead of poverty, an end to the scourge of violence, support for working families, and the closing of the gender wage gap.

- By 2020 our dreams can come true: women as partners in policy making, womenomics as an accepted fact, a revitalized social compact, young women growing up expecting to be leaders, and accountability mechanisms in place.

Dream #1: Women leaders are at every political table to assure the needed changes in systems and institutions. We have reached the tipping point nationally as well as in the fifty states and are approaching parity for women in political leadership.

We can begin simply by making sure every single open seat has a woman candidate who shares our values. Political parties and activists can expand recruitment and training of women candidates and help raise the necessary resources. Insider women can proudly initiate action to get more women elected or appointed. When they move up the career ladder or leave politics, they can mentor and champion other women to take their places.

We can also set standards for women's representation and invest in accomplishing the goal of reaching critical mass. In doing this we can look to the experience of other countries that have taken the lead. Despite the U.S. aversion to such standards, they are the most effective approach and can be set voluntarily at any level, though mandatory nationwide standards would be the most effective.

Dream #2: Womenomics is a widely supported mainstream strategy to grow a productive, competitive economy. Boards and top management have at least 30% women. Women are seen as expected (rather than unusual) leaders.

Models and pilot projects already exist. We'll know our vision has become conventional wisdom when most businesses look like today's *Working Mother* family-friendly awardees, placing a heavy premium on human capital, diversity, equity, teamwork, innovation, flexibility, creativity, and collaboration. We'll be there when the standard elements of the economic infrastructure go beyond roads and bridges to include early care and education and support services for working families. We'll be there when investors put their money in socially responsible companies with a strong record of women's advancement and shun others as poor investments for the long term. Women's entrepreneurship will be recognized as an important economic sector, and gender-related barriers halting start-ups or growth plans will have disappeared. A focus on womenomics will promote economic self-sufficiency for women, provide impetus for raising the minimum wage and equal pay, and clear the way for women, including single moms, to be able to support their families.

Dream #3: *A revitalized social compact places a premium on social and personal responsibility, caring and compassion, families, and community.*

We'll be there when the women-centered caring professions have long-overdue salary increases commensurate with the cost-benefit evidence of their importance to society. Excellent research shows, for example, that having enough well-prepared nurses is essential to good patient outcomes and saves money. And Nobel Prize–winning economists have shown that investment in early care and education pays off in a lifetime of learning for our children, but income levels for teachers have to be high enough to attract and retain the very best qualified.

We'll be there when "giving back" is expected from everyone to make our shared quality of life better and when being a caring member of a community and family is valued and expected of all successful people—men and women alike.

Dream #4: *A recognized accountability framework of standards and measurements exists to monitor progress, assure open*

opportunity, close the gaps, and tap the skills and leadership
capacity of women as well as men.

We will know we are there when the United States has ratified and implemented the Women's Treaty (CEDAW), which was signed by President Carter in 1980. Only a tiny handful of countries have not ratified it already. President Obama and Secretary of State Hillary Clinton have called for the Senate finally to approve this treaty.[17] It provides a set of tools and standards for the country to evaluate where it is on women's advancement and hold itself accountable for continued progress.

We'll really assure continued progress when an Insider approach including more women public officials, passage of CEDAW, and a White House Council on Women and Girls is complemented by an Outsider approach. A "Women at the Top Compact" including the leading women in government, business, academia, media, the nonprofit sector, and religious institutions would be a powerful network to help more women advance to leadership positions and hold officials accountable. This Inside-Outside model could be replicated at the local or state level to carry the message, "I made it, and so can you!"

Dream #5: Young women grow up expecting to be leaders,
just like young men—but with a difference.

When "command and control" leadership styles are replaced by a focus on ethics, personal principles, and social change values, we'll be there. Then we will be meeting the girls' definition in a Girl Scout study appropriately called "Change It Up! What Girls Say about Redefining Leadership." Girls will be as likely as boys to want to be leaders (now at least half of girls of color express such interest, compared to only one-third of Caucasian girls).[18] We'll no longer be reading reports of the "girl box," the dropping back of creative and talented middle school girls from their dreams and their studies to gain popularity. Instead, programs to improve lifetime self-esteem, like Girls on the Run, now training girls as runners in 157 cities to promote a positive self-image, will be commonplace.[19]

This Week I Will . . .

✔ Start a list of the hopes and dreams I share with other women about the future for the children of today.

✔ Begin to think about how we can get enough women at the table to try to make one of my dreams come true by 2020.

✔ Invite some family and friends to a kitchen-table conversation about the next steps to see that more girls and women are ready to move up.

✔ Use the information here to check the status of my state on women in the economy and politics and share it with my networks—and challenge them to act.

We'll have reached our goal when learning opportunities for leadership are widely available for women and girls of all ages. The Public Leadership Education Network, composed of sixteen colleges and universities, is now twenty-five years old and prepares college women to make a difference in the public policy world with extensive educational and internship programs as well as access to a powerful network of women leaders. Columbia College in Columbia, South Carolina, a liberal arts women's college, has infused leadership into its curriculum and expects every student to consciously examine and expand her leadership potential before graduation. The students I met in a focus group at the college were proud of their newfound leadership ability and ready to lead.[20] When we've reached our goal, there will be more programs like these in more places.

• • •

Having more women leaders matters—a lot—because it works. As you and many other women step into leadership, we will have enough women making decisions to cause a wave of change and make our dreams come true. Each of us can personify the 4Cs leadership taught at Columbia College: we can shine with *courage*, show *commitment* to our personal goals, step out with *confidence*, and strive for *competence* to make a difference.

We will change the systems that fail to reflect our views, values, and experience. We will use our power to work with like-minded men and change the world. As transformational leaders, we can make life better for ourselves, for generations of girls and boys coming behind us, and for society. Women will lead the way as primary economic actors and energizers for civic and political change.

Notes

Note: The URLs in this section were verified in January 2009.

Preface

1. Informal focus groups were held with women executives in finance in Chicago and New York City; corporate women executives (from around the country) in Washington, DC; college students at Columbia College, Columbia, South Carolina; grantees of the Washington Area Women's Foundation in Washington, DC; working mothers with children in preschool in Fort Myers, Florida; young women activists in New York City; leaders of organizations representing women-owned businesses in Washington, DC; women in philanthropy in Denver; women community activists in Chicago; national experts on women, development, and violence in Washington, DC; and the editors of the *American Journal of Nursing* in New York City.

Introduction

1. Nicholas Kristof, "Mistresses of the Universe," *New York Times*, February 8, 2009, http://www.nytimes.com/2009/02/08/opinion/08kristof.html?_r=1.
2. See the Resources section of this book for examples.
3. Ruth Marcus, "Wanted: Justices from Venus," *Washington Post*, May 12, 2009, http://www.washingtonpost.com/wp-dyn/content/article/2009/05/12/AR20090 51202879.html.
4. Deborah L. Rhode, ed., *The Difference "Difference" Makes: Women and Leadership* (Stanford, CA: Stanford University Press, 2003).

5. Pamela Paxton and Melanie M. Hughes, *Women, Politics, and Power: A Global Perspective* (Thousand Oaks, CA: Pine Forge Press, 2007), 207–8. The four categories identified by Rosabeth Moss Kanter in her 1977 book *Men, Women and the Corporation* (New York: Basic Books, 1977) are (1) uniform groups with only one type of person (e.g., 100% men, 0% women); (2) skewed groups with mostly one type of person (e.g., 85% men , 15% women); (3) tilted groups moving toward balance (e.g., 65% men, 35% women); and (4) parity groups with equal numbers.

6. Linda Tarr-Whelan, "Women's Voices 1992, 1995, 1996, 2000," Center for Policy Alternatives. The organization is no longer in business. The polls were done by a bipartisan, multicultural team led by Celinda Lake (Democrat) and Linda DiVall (Republican). Later polls done by a number of organizations have affirmed this work.

7. Anna Quindlen, "The Value of the Outsider," *Newsweek*, October 24, 2005, http://www.newsweek.com/id/50729/page/1.

8. Bill George, "Truly Authentic Leadership," blog posting in *U.S. News and World Report*, October 22, 2006, http://www.usnews.com/usnews/news/articles/061022/30authentic_print.htm.

9. Marie Wilson, *Closing the Leadership Gap: Why Women Can and Must Help Run the World* (New York: Viking Penguin, 2004), xvi. The subtitle of the new paperback edition is *Add Women, Change Everything*.

Chapter 1

1. Fortune 500 2008, "Women CEOs," http://money.cnn.com/magazines/fortune/fortune500/2008/womenceos/.

2. Brainy Quotes, "Eleanor Rosevelt Quotes," http://www.brainyquote.com/quotes/quotes/e/eleanorroo128066.html.

3. UN Division for the Advancement of Women, Fourth World Conference on Women, http://www.un.org/womenwatch/daw/beijing/platform/index.html.

4. Inter-Parlimentary Union, "Women in National Parliments," http://www.ipu.org/wmn-e/classif.htm.

5. Similarly, at the end of World War II, the American Occupation in Japan wrote the Equal Rights Amendment into the new Japanese constitution, although it still has not been adopted in the United States. It can be found in Article 14: http://www.servat.unibe.ch/icl/ja00000_.html.

6. Chandra Mudaliar, "India's Gender Reservation Policy and Women's Emerging Political Leadership at the Grassroots"(presentation, American Political Science Association, September 1, 2005), http://www.allacademic.com//meta/p_mla_apa _research_citation/0/4/1/2/6.

7. Margaret Alva, general secretary of the All India Congress Committee, former minister and the drafter of the legislation when she was in Parliament, at Salzburg Global Seminar, September 2006, based on government reports.

8. About.com: Women's History, "Women Prime Ministers and Presidents—20th Century Heads of State," http://womenshistory.about.com/od/rulers20th/(null).htm.

9. Susan Carroll, *The Impact of Women in Public Office* (Bloomington: Indiana University Press, 2001); Center for American Women and Politics, "Women State Legislators: Past, Present and Future," http://www.cawp.rutgers.edu/research/topics/documents/StLeg2001Report.pdf. Earlier research is reported by Sue Thomas, *How Women Legislate* (New York: Oxford University Press, 1994) and Cindy Simon Rosenthal, *When Women Lead: Integrative Leadership in State Legislatures* (New York: Oxford University Press, 1998).

10. Barbara Boxer, *Strangers in the Senate: Politics and the New Revolution of Women in America* (Washington, DC: National Press Books, 1994), 32.

11. Lois Joy et al., "The Bottom Line: Corporate Performance and Women's Representation on Boards," Catalyst, October 2007, http://www.catalyst.org/publication/200/the-bottom-line-corporate-performance-and-womens-representation-on-boards.

12. Georges Desvaux et al., "A Business Case for Women," *McKinsey Quarterly*, September 2008, http://www.mckinseyquarterly.com/A_business_case_for_women_2192.

13. Kevin Sullivan and Mary Jordan, "Another Mess to Clean Up: Europe Seeks Women to Control Purse Strings," *Washington Post* National Weekly Edition, February 16–22, 2009, 19.

14. More information and an annual report are available at http://www.deloitte.com/dtt/article/0,1002,sid=108843&cid=248971,00.html?wt.mc_id=IWD.

15. Conference notes at New York City event sponsored by UNIFEM, Verité, and Calvert Funds.

16. Lois Joy, "Advancing Women Leaders: The Connection between Women Board Directors and Women Corporate Officers," Catalyst, July 2008, http://www.catalyst.org/publication/273/advancing-women-leaders-the-connection-between-women-board-directors-and-women-corporate-officers.

17. Mary O'Hara Devereaux, speech to annual meeting of Corporate Voices for Working Families, June 5, 2007.

18. Comparison of the World Economic Forum's Global Gender Gap Report and its Global Competitiveness Report for 2008, http://www.wef.org/.

19. Hillary Clinton, quoted by Dana Milbank in the *Washington Post*, http://www.washingtonpost.com/wp-dyn/content/article/2008/06/07/AR2008060701879.html.

20. Georges Desvaux et al., "A Business Case for Women," *McKinsey Quarterly*, September 2008, http://www.mckinseyquarterly.com/A_business_case_for_women _2192.

21. Center for American Women and Politics, "Women Candidates for US Congress, 1974–2008," Fast Facts, http://www.cawp.rutgers.edu/fast_facts/elections/ documents/canwincong_histsum.pdf.

Chapter 2

1. "This Is a Man's World," *Economist*, September 8, 2008, at http://www.economist. com.

2. Women's Media Center, "Sexism Sells, but We're Not Buying It," http://www .womensmediacenter.com/sexism_sells.html.

3. Neela Banerjeee, "Clergywomen Find a Hard Path to Bigger Pulpit," *New York Times*, August 26, 2008, http://www.nytimes.com/2006/08/26/us/26clergy.html ?_r=2&pagewanted=1&en=ea5f1&hp&ex=1156651200.

4. Nicholas Kristof, "When Women Rule," *New York Times,* February 10, 2008, http://www.nytimes.com/2008/02/10/opinion/10kristof.html.

5. Catalyst, "The Double-Bind Dilemma for Women in Leadership: Damned If You Do, Doomed If You Don't," 2007, http://www.catalyst.org/publication/83/ the-double-bind-dilemma-for-women-in-leadership-damned-if-you-do-doomed -if-you-dont.

6. Ibid.

7. Tom Toles Cartoons, January 9, 2008, *Washington Post*, http://www.washington post.com/wp-srv/opinions/cartoonsandvideos/toles_main.html.

8. Catalyst, "Damned or Doomed."

9. "Milestones," *Time*, August 21, 2006, http://www.time.com/time/magazine/ article/0,9171,1229207.00.html.

10. Catalyst, "Damned or Doomed."

11. Kathleen Hall Jamieson, *Beyond the Double Bind: Women and Leadership* (New York: Oxford University Press, 1995), 7.

12. Catalyst, "Women and Men in US Corporate Leadership: Same Workplace, Different Realities?" fact sheet, 2004.

13. Arlie Hochschild, *Inside the Clockwork of Male Careers*, quoted in National Academy of Sciences, "From Scarcity to Visibility: Gender Differences in the Careers of Doctoral Scientists and Engineers," 2001, http://www.books.nap.edu/ openbook.php?record_id=5363&page=1.htm.

14. Families and Work Institute, "25-Year Trend Data Facts," http://familiesandwork .org/site/comparedata.html.

15. Sylvia Ann Hewlett, *Off-Ramps and On-Ramps* (Cambridge: Harvard Business School Press, 2007).

16. Jason Fields, "Children's Living Arrangements and Characteristics," Current Population Reports 20-547, March 2002 Current Population Survey, U.S. Census Bureau, issued June 2003.

17. Ellen Goodman, "Workplace Rules Make Mothers a Third Gender," *Boston Globe*, May 11, 2007.

18. Sam Roberts, "For Young Earners in Big City, a Gap in Women's Favor," *New York Times*, August 3, 2007.

19. E. J. Graff, "The Mommy War Machine," *Washington Post Outlook*, April 29, 2007.

Chapter 3

1. U.S. Department of Education, "Trends in Educational Equity of Girls and Women: 2004," http://nces.ed.gov/pubs2005/equity/.

2. Families and Work Institute, "25-Year Trend Data Facts from the National Study of the Changing Workforce," http://familiesandwork.org/site/comparedata.html.

3. U.S. Census Bureau, "Facts for Features: Women's History Month," January 4, 2007, and February 22, 2005, http://www.census.gov/Press-Release/www/releases/archives/facts_for_features_special_editions.htm.

4. Center for Women's Business Research, "Key Facts about Women-Owned Businesses," http://www.cfwbr.org/facts/index/php.

5. International Monetary Fund, "World Economic and Financial Surveys: World Economic Outlook Database," September 2006, http://www.imf.org/external/pubs/ft/weo/2006/02/data/weorept.aspx?sy=2003&ey=2007.

6. Laura Tyson, Saadia Zahidi, and Ricardo Hausmann, "The Global Gender Gap Report 2008," World Economic Forum, http://www.weforum.org/pdf/gendergap/rankings2008.pdf.

7. "Women in Elective Office 2007," Center for American Women and Politics, Eagleton Institute, Rutgers University, http://www.cawp.rutgers.edu.

8. "Women Achieve Record Numbers in State Legislatures, . . ." press release issued by Center for American Women and Politics, Rutgers University, November 11, 2008. http://www.cawp.rutgers.edu/press_room/news/documents/PressRelease_11-11-08.pdf.

9. Inter-Parliamentary Union, "Women in National Parliaments," as of November 30, 2006, http://www.ipu.org/wmn-e/classif.htm.

10. "I Am Woman, Hear Me Shop," *Business Week* Special Report, February 14, 2005, http://www.businessweek.com/bwdaily/dnflash/feb2005/nf20050214 _9413_db_082.htm.

11. Jody Heymann et al., *The Work, Family and Equity Index: How Does the United States Measure Up?* Project on Global Working Families of the Institute of Health and Social Policy, McGill University, 2007.

12. AngloINFO, "Having a Baby in Portugal," http://algarve.angloinfo.com/countries/ portugal/birth.asp.

13. Catalyst, "2006 Census of Women Corporate Officers, Top Earners, and Directors of the Fortune 500," press release, February 21, 2007.

14. Heidi Hartmann, "The Gender Gap Is Real: Economic Policy Institute Snapshots," http://epi.org/content.cfm/webfeatures_snapshots_20050914.

15. Corporate Voices for Working Families, "Workplace Flexibility for Lower-Wage Workers," October 2006, 9 (http://www.cvworkingfamilies.org/).

Chapter 4

1. Hannah Seligson, "Girl Power in School but Not in the Office," *New York Times,* August 13, 2008, http://www.nytimes.com/2008/08/31/jobs/31pre.html.

2. Myra Hart, quoted in Seligson, "Girl Power."

3. Linda C. Babcock, professor of economics at Carnegie Mellon University, teamed up with writer Sara Laschever for *Women Don't Ask: Negotiation and the Gender Divide* (Princeton, NJ: Princeton University Press, 2003), which has been followed by a number of articles and a new book, *Ask for It: How Women Can Use the Power of Negotiation to Get What They Really Want* (New York: Bantam, 2009).

4. Laura Liswood, secretary-general of the Council of Women World Leaders, opening address at Salzburg Global Seminar, November 2007. More information is provided at http://www.womenworldleaders.org.

5. Prudential Financial, 2008–2009 study, "Financial Experience and Behaviors among Women," http://www.prudential.com/media/managed/2006WomenBrochure _FINAL.pdf.

6. Michelle Singletary, "The Color of Money: More Confidence Would Help Women Meet Financial Goals," *Rutland (VT) Daily Herald,* September 1, 2008, C3.

Chapter 5

1. Kevin Sullivan and Mary Jordan, "In Banking Crisis, Guys Get the Blame: More Women Needed in Top Jobs, Critics Say," *Washington Post,* February 11, 2009, http://www.washingtonpost.com/wp-dyn/content/article/2009/02/10/AR20090 21002398.html.

2. Nicholas Kristof, "Mistresses of the Universe," *New York Times,* February 7, 2009, http://www.nytimes.com/2009/02/08/opinion/08kristof.html?_r=1.

3. Foon Rhee, "Obama Creates Women's Council," March 11, 2009, http://www .boston.com/news/politics/politicalintelligence/2009/03/obama_creates_w.html.

4. Sally Helgesen, *The Female Advantage: Women's Ways of Leadership* (New York: Currency Doubleday, 1990).

5. Dorothy W. Cantor and Toni Bernay, *Women in Power: The Secrets of Leadership* (Boston: Houghton Mifflin, 1992).

6. Joe Nocera, "Running G.E., Comfortable in His Skin," *New York Times,* June 9, 2007.

7. Informal focus group, October 10, 2007, Chicago.

8. Amartya Sen, Special Irene Tinker Lecture Series, International Council for Research on Women, October 11, 2006, http://www.icrw.org/html/specialevents/ 06-tinker-amartyasen.htm.

9. Somini Sengupta, "An Empire for Poor Working Women, Guided by a Gandhian Approach," *New York Times,* March 7, 2009.

10. "World Bank Issue Brief/Gender Equality," October 19, 2007, 1.

11. "The Status of South Carolina Women," commissioned from the Moore School of Business, University of South Carolina, by the SC Alliance for Women, 2006, http://www.allianceforwomen.net/public/pdf/FullReport_2006.pdf.

Chapter 6

1. Informal focus group of 12 twenty- and thirty-something women community activists, March 8, 2007.

2. Bruce Japsen, "More Women Move into Top Jobs at Health Insurers," *Chicago Tribune,* February 15, 2008.

3. Facts and Figures on Violence against Women, in UNIFEM, "Say No to Violence against Women," http://www.unifem.org/campaigns/vaw/facts_figures.php?=7.

4. Joanna Barsh, Susie Cranston, and Rebecca A. Craske, "Centered Leadership: How Talented Women Thrive," *McKinsey Quarterly,* September 2008, http://www .mckinseyquarterly.com/Centered_leadership_How_talented_women_thrive_ 2193.

5. Sylvia Hewlett, *Off-Ramps and On-Ramps: Keeping Talented Women on the Road to Success* (Cambridge: Harvard University Press, 2007).

6. Sara Horowitz, interview by the author, December 5, 2007, New York City. For additional information, see http://www.freelancersunion.org.

7. Zeyba Rahman, interview by the author, December 4, 2007, New York City. For additional information, see http://www.junglibilli.com.

8. Connie Evans, interview by the author, October 10, 2007, Chicago.

9. Noeleen Heyzer, interview by the author, October 30, 2006, New York City. For further information, see http://www.UNIFEM.org.

Chapter 7

1. Karen Medhurst and Juanita Edenfield were the Orangewood teachers.

2. Legal Momentum, "Reading between the Lines: Women's Poverty in the United States, 2003," fact sheet, October 2004.

3. American Heart Association, http://www.americanheart.org/presenter.jhtml ?identifier=3053.

4. Marie Wilson, "Adding Women Changes Everything at *Meet the Press*," blog posting on the Huffington Post, October 23, 2007.

5. Research and Stats section of the Women's Media Center website, http://www .womensmediacenter.com/research.html.

6. Catalyst and the Families and Work Institute, "Leaders in a Global Economy: Finding the Fit for Top Talent," May 2008, http://familiesandwork.org/site/news room/releases/globaltalentmgmt.html.

7. Washington Area Women's Foundation, "A Portrait of Women and Girls in the Washington Metro Area," 2003, http://thewomensfoundation.org/images/ PortraitFinal.pdf.

8. The Center for Policy Alternatives, which conducted this series of polls, is no longer in business. Some reports of the 1992 poll (done with the Ms. Foundation) and the 2000 poll (with Lifetime Television) are still available online at http:// www.stateaction.org/, www.commondreams.org/, and http://www.fordfound .org/. The author directed this work and relied upon personal papers.

9. Women's Voices, Women Vote website, http://wvwv.org/.

10. "I Am Woman, Hear Me Shop," *Business Week* Special Report, February 14, 2005, http://www.businessweek.com/bwdaily/dnflash/feb2005/nf20050214 _9413_db_082.htm.

11. Andrea Learned, "The Six Costliest Mistakes You Can Make in Marketing to Women," ReachWomen, http://www.inc.com/articles/2003/01/25019.html.

12. First reported on MSNBC, August 13, 2006. Allianz, "Women, Money and Power," press release, http://www.allianzlife.com/WomenMoneyPower/Default.aspx.

13. *Wall Street Week with Fortune*, PBS, July 11, 2006, http://www.pbs.org/wsw/ tvprogram/20050617merrillsurvey.html.

14. Calvert Investments, "Special Report: Calvert Women's Principles," http://www .calvert.com/womensPrinciples.html.

15. Pax World Women's Equity Fund, http://www.paxworld.com/funds/womens -equity-fund/.

16. Ibid.

Chapter 8

1. Rosabeth Moss Kanter, Ernest L. Arbuckle Professor at Harvard Business School, quoted in "Do Women Make a Difference?" in Pamela Paxton and Melanie M. Hughes, *Women, Power and Politics: A Global Perspective* (Thousand Oaks, CA: Pine Forge Press, 2007), 208.

2. Joanna Barsh, Susie Cranston, and Rebecca A. Craske, "Centered Leadership: How Talented Women Thrive," *McKinsey Quarterly*, September 2008, http://www .mckinseyquarterly.com/Centered_leadership_How_talented_women_thrive_ 2193.

3. Rachel L. Swarns, "Obamas and Clinton Honor Women," *New York Times*, March 11, 2009, http://thecaucus.blogs.nytimes.com/2009/03/11/obamas-and -clinton-honor-women/?pagem.

4. Valerie Jarrett, interview by Linda Wertheimer, *NPR Morning Edition*, March 12, 2009.

5. Judith Lichtman, conversation with author, March 20, 2006.

6. "Employer Study from Families and Work Institute Shows Significant Changes for U.S. Workers since 1998," press release issued by Families and Work Institute, May 2008, http://familiesandwork.org/site/newsroom/releases/2008nse.html.

7. Corporate Voices for Working Families, "Workforce Flexibility," http://www .corporatevoices.org/our-work/workplace-flexibility.

8. Ibid.

9. Informal focus group with women corporate executives, Washington, DC, June 4, 2007.

10. Virginia Littlejohn, CEO, Quantum Leaps, Inc., interview by the author, May 10, 2006.

Chapter 9

1. Barbara Krumsiek, CEO of Calvert Funds, in numerous meetings in 2006, when I was a consultant.

2. Marilyn Davidson and Ronald J. Burk, eds., *Women in Management Worldwide: Facts, Figures and Analyses* (Aldershot, UK: Ashgate Publishing, 2004).

3. Patricia Deyton et al., "Survey: Many Women Aspire to For-Profit Board Membership," press release issued by Simmons School of Management, Boston, March 31, 2008, http://management.simmons.edu/som/news/3159.shtml.

4. Gwladys Fouché and Jill Treanor, "In Norway, a Woman's Place Is in the Board-room: Firms Must Introduce Female Directors or Face Closure under a New Law," *Guardian*, January 9, 2006, http://www.guardian.co.uk/money/2006/jan/09/business.workandcareers.

5. Alison Maitland, "A Step Up for Senior Women," *Financial Times*, October 8, 2008, http://us.ft.com/ftgateway/superpage.ft?news_id=fto100820081738005134&page=2.

6. For more information on this topic, see Miki Caul Kittilson, *Challenging Parties, Changing Parliament: Women and Elected Office in Contemporary Parliaments and Legislatures* (Columbus Ohio State University Press, 2006).

7. Fact sheets for 2008, Center for American Women in Politics, Eagleton Institute, Rutgers University, http://www.cawp.rutgers.edu/.

8. Ann Fisher, quoted in the Midwest Edition of The White House Project e-mail list serv, "Achieving Gender Parity in Ohio," http://twhp.convio.net/site/MessageViewer?em_id=1361.0.

9. "Appointed Policy Makers in State Government: Glass Ceiling in Gubernatorial Appointments, 1997–2007," Center for Women in Government and Civil Society, University at Albany, State University of New York, Summer 2008.

Chapter 10

1. Alex Williams, "That Business Card Won't Fly Here," *New York Times*, Sunday Styles, October 26, 2008, 2.

2. Joanna Barsh, Susie Cranston, and Rebecca A. Craske, "Centered Leadership: How Talented Women Thrive," *McKinsey Quarterly*, September 2008, http://www.mckinseyquarterly.com/Centered_leadership_How_talented_women_thrive_2193.

3. Allison H. Fine, *Momentum: Igniting Social Change in the Connected Age* (San Francisco: Jossey-Bass, 2006), 60.

4. "Kuwait Set to Give Women the Vote," BBC News, April 19, 2005, http://news.bbc.co.uk/2/hi/middle_east/4460781.stm.

5. "Woman Elected in Kuwait Says Gender in Politics Is 'History,'" CNN.com, May 17, 2009, http://www.cnn.com/2009/WORLD/meast/05/17/kuwait.women.elections/index.html?eref=rss_latest.

6. Focus group, October 10, 2006, Chicago.

7. Swanee Hunt, *Half-Life of a Zealot* (Durham, NC: Duke University Press, 2006), 164–71.

8. Focus group, March 6, 2006, Denver.

9. Focus group, October 11, 2006, Evanston, Illinois.

10. Women Leading Kentucky, http://www.womenleadingky.com/ and Janet Holloway, conversation with author, October 16, 2007.

11. Focus group, October 16, 2007, Lexington, Kentucky.
12. Center for Policy Alternatives, "Women Win Battle: Thank You, Viagra," *Ways and Means,* Summer 2000. Jackie Speier is now a member of Congress.
13. Carey Goldberg, "Insurance for Viagra Spurs Coverage for Birth Control," *New York Times,* June 30, 1999.
14. Linda Tarr-Whelan, "Policy and Politics: Sick Leave Anyone," *American Journal of Nursing,* September 2007, 37–39.
15. A summary of recent research is found in Daniel Sitter, "Presenteeism: The Hidden Cost of Doing Business," *Ezine,* 2008, http://ezinearticles.com/?Presenteeism:-The-Hidden-Costs-of-Business&id=40408.
16. Infoplease, "The Wage Gap," http://www.infoplease.com/ipa/A0763170.html.
17. "Pay Discrimination: Ledbetter v. Goodyear," *New York Times,* http://www.nytimes.com/ref/washington/scotuscases_PAYDISCRIMINATION.html.

Conclusion

1. National Portrait Gallery, Smithsonian Institution, "The Seneca Falls Convention, July, 19–20, 1848," http://www.npg.si.edu/col/seneca/senfalls1.htm.
2. Kathy Bonk and Linda Tarr-Whelan, "The Global Journey toward Women's Empowerment: A New Frame," in *Global Women's Empowerment: A Call for a New Framework for Women, Work and Development,* Communications Consortium Media Center report commissioned by the Rockefeller Foundation, 2002.
3. Ibid.
4. All salary figures are from 2006 from PayScale, http://www.payscale.com/research/US/Job/Salary.
5. Leonard Masse and W. Steven Barnett, "A Benefit-Cost Analysis of Abecedarian Early Childhood Intervention," National Institute for Early Education Research Hot Topics, 2009, http://nieer.org/docs/?DocID=57. This is the most recent of a long series of research reports showing between 4:1 and 7:1 return on money spent for high-quality early childhood education programs.
6. Further information is available at http://www.doingbusiness.org/, http://www.worldbank.org/gender and http://www.ifc.org/gender. Amanda Ellis can be reached at aellis@worldbank.org.
7. Goldman Sachs, "Goldman Sachs Launches 10,000 Women," press release, March 8, 2008, and Global Economics paper no. 164, "Women Hold Up Half the Sky," by Sandra Lawson, March 4, 2008.
8. Elizabeth Olson, "Business Skills for Women Overseas: A Way to Bolster Emerging Markets," *New York Times,* December 26, 2008, B3.
9. Sara Gould, president of the Ms. Foundation, conversation with author, May 1, 2006.

10. Anne Mosle, conversation with author, March 20, 2006.

11. World Economic Forum, "Global Gender Gap Report 2008," http://www.we forum.org/en/Communities/Women Leaders and Gender Parity/GenderGap Network/index.htm.

12. Ibid.

13. The only similar state-by-state economic benchmarking exercise in the United States is done by the Institute for Women's Policy Research (http://www.iwpr .org/) on earnings, the gender wage gap, the percentage of women in managerial/ professional occupations, business ownership, and poverty rates. IWPR also has some more detailed reports for certain states. Some excellent studies of women's advancement in particular cities and states have been done by women's funds and foundations. You can find the fund in your area through the member directory of the Women's Funding Network (http://www.womensfundingnetwork.org/). The Center for American Women and Politics (CAWP), part of the Eagleton Institute at Rutgers University (http://www.cawp.rutgers.edu/), compiles detailed information about women's political representation, including state-by-state data. Catalyst (http://www.catalyst.org/), the organization dedicated to opening opportunities for women in business, has excellent data on women decision makers in various fields.

14. "CEDAW in San Francisco: From International Human Rights to Local Policies for Women," in International Museum for Women, *Women, Power and Politics,* http://www.imow.org/wpp/stories/viewStory?storyId=1849.

15. "A Guide to Womenomics," *Economist,* April 12, 2006, http://www.economist .com/finance/displaystory.cfm?story_id=E1_GRDNVVT.

16. "Womenomics Revisited," *Economist,* April 19, 2007, http://www.economist.com/ finance/displaystory.cfm?story_id=9038760.

17. For further information and how you can help, see http://www.womenstreaty.org/.

18. "Transforming Leadership: Focus on Outcomes of the New Girl Scout Leadership Experience," Girl Scouts of America, 2008, http://www.girlscouts.org/ research/publications/outcomes/transforming_leadership.asp.

19. Molly Barker, *Girls on Track: A Parent's Guide to Inspiring Our Daughters to Achieve a Lifetime of Self-Esteem and Respect* (New York: Ballantine Books, 2004). For more information, see http://www.girlsontherun.org/.

20. Caroline Whitson, president of Columbia College, interview by the author, July 27, 2006; http://www.columbiacollegesc.edu/leadership; and focus group with students, September 24, 2007.

Resources

*This part of the book provides you with additional sources of information,
including books and the websites of organizations and networks. It is arranged
by chapter. Note: The URLs in this section were verified in January 2009.*

Preface: The Story behind the Book

*Biographies and histories of women who have made a real difference continue
to be a source of inspiration to me. Here are just a few of my favorites:*

Chesler, Ellen. *Woman of Valor: Margaret Sanger and the Birth Control Movement in America.* New York: Simon & Schuster, 2007.

Collins, Gail. *America's Women: 400 Years of Dolls, Drudges, Helpmates and Heroines.* New York: William Morrow, 2003.

Cook, Blanche Wiesen. *Eleanor Roosevelt.* Vol. 1, *1884–1933.* New York: Penguin Books, 1992.

Graham, Katharine. *Personal History.* New York: Random House, 1997.

Griffith, Elisabeth. *The Life of Elizabeth Cady Stanton.* New York: Oxford University Press, 1984.

Howard, Jane. *Margaret Mead: A Life.* New York: Ballantine Books, 1984.

Knight, Louise W. *Jane Addams and the Struggle for Democracy.* Chicago: University of Chicago Press, 2006.

Levine, Suzanne Braun, and Mary Thom. *Bella Abzug: How One Tough Broad from the Bronx Fought Jim Crow and Joe McCarthy, Pissed Off Jimmy Carter,*

Battled for the Rights of Women and Workers, Rallied against War and for the Planet, and Shook Up Politics All the Way. New York: Farrar, Straus and Giroux, 2007.

Introduction: More Women Leaders, Better Leadership

Some of the useful books and websites on women's leadership (in addition to the books by Marie Wilson and Deborah Rhode listed in the endnotes) include:

Cantor, Dorothy W., and Toni Bernay. *Women in Power: The Secrets of Leadership*. New York: Houghton Mifflin, 1992.

Coughlin, Linda, Ellen Wingard, and Keith Hollihan, eds. *Enlightened Power: How Women Are Transforming the Practice of Leadership*. San Francisco: Jossey-Bass, 2005.

Donlan, Vicki, with Helen French Graves. *Her Turn: Why It's Time for Women to Lead in America*. Westport, CT: Praeger, 2007.

Eagley, Alice H., and Linda L. Carli. *Through the Labyrinth: The Truth about How Women Become Leaders*. Boston: Harvard Business School Press, 2007.

Frankel, Lois. *See Jane Lead: 99 Ways for Women to Take Charge at Work*. New York: Warner Business Books, 2007.

The Global Women's Leadership Network at Santa Clara University is led by Linda Alepin at http://www.scu.edu/business/gwln/.

Hartman, Mary S., ed. *Talking Leadership: Conversations with Powerful Women*. New Brunswick, NJ: Rutgers University Press, 1999.

Helgesen, Sally. *Everyday Revolutionaries: Working Women and the Transformation of American Life*. New York: Bantam Doubleday Dell, 1998.

Kellerman, Barbara, and Deborah L. Rhode, eds. *Women and Leadership: The State of Play and Strategies for Change*. San Francisco: Jossey-Bass, 2007.

Kunin, Madeleine M. *Pearls, Politics, and Power*. White River Junction, VT: Chelsea Green Publishing, 2008.

Myers, Dee Dee. *Why Women Should Rule the World*. New York: Harper Collins, 2008.

Wittenberg-Cox, Avivah, and Alison Maitland. *Why Women Mean Business: Understanding the Emergence of Our Next Economic Revolution*. West Sussex, England: John Wiley & Sons, 2008.

Avivah Wittenberg-Cox has established a one-stop location for new business information globally at http://20-first.com.

Chapter 1: The 30% Solution

See endnotes. The websites for organizations mentioned in the chapter are:

Beijing Platform for Action, http://www.un.org/womenwatch/daw/beijing/platform .index.html

Catalyst, headed by Ilene Lang: http://www.catalyst.org/

Center for American Women and Politics, Eagleton Institute, Rutgers University, led by Debbie Walsh: http://www.cawp.rutgers.edu/

Inter-Parliamentary Union: http://www.ipu.org/

The White House Project, led by Marie Wilson: http://www.thewhitehouseproject .org/

The Women's Media Center, headed by Carol Jenkins: http://www.womensmedia center.com/

Chapter 2: Modern Myths and Stereotypes

See endnotes.

Chapter 3: The Everywoman Quiz

See endnotes.

Chapter 4: Breaking Out of the Box

Laura Liswood's interviews with women world leaders are available in book and DVD form. They give you a wonderful picture of how women can have varied leadership styles (the leaders include Margaret Thatcher, Gro Harlem Brundtland, and others) yet be forceful figures bringing women's views and values to the table. They can be found through the Aspen Institute publications at http://www.aspeninstitute.org/publications. The Council for Women World Leaders is headquartered there as well, and you can see its work at http:// www.womenworldleaders.org/.

Chapter 5: Today's Transformational Leader

For further information about the UN conferences and international progress for women, see the websites of UNIFEM (http://www.unifem.org/) and the Commission on the Status of Women (http://www.un.org/womenwatch/daw/csw/).

To learn more about microfinance investments in the United States and abroad, check out the Microcredit Summit Campaign at http://www.microcredit summit.org/ and the Association for Enterprise Opportunity, headed by Connie Evans, at http://www.microenterpriseworks.org/.

Women-led initiatives are leading to positive change, although often women are still talking only to women rather than being able to influence the wider debate.

- *Women's foundations are leading the way on new strategies to help poor families move up. The Women's Funding Network, led by Christine Grumm, includes information and a list of the more than one hundred women's funds at http://www.womensfundingnetwork.org/.*

- *Entrepreneurial women are creating jobs and companies quite successfully. Julie Weeks, a real expert in this area, has created her own consultancy, Womenable. On the website you will find excellent quarterly newsletters (http://www.womenable.com/). The National Women's Business Council is a federal advisory group and has excellent resources (http://www.nwbc.gov/).*

- *Women's organizations are working to connect women in the global South and North. Several excellent groups have information for you and connections to the work. They include Women Thrive Worldwide, headed by Ritu Sharma (http://www.womensedge.org/), and the International Center for Research on Women, led by Geeta Rao Gupta (http://www.icrw.org/).*

- *Nursing research to improve patient outcomes and cut costs is important to the future of the health care debate. Resources include the National Institutes of Health program (http://www.ninr.nih.gov/); the American Academy of Nursing, headed by Pat Ford-Roegner (http://www.aannet.org/); and various nursing journals, including the* American Journal of Nursing, *with Diana Mason as executive editor.*

Chapter 6: Starting Right Here, Right Now

To understand more about women in peacekeeping and reconstruction, see the website of the Women's International League for Peace and Freedom, "Peace Women," at http://www.peacewomen.org/un/sc/1325.html.

Project Vote Smart: http://www.votesmart.org/

Chapter 7: Making Women's Power Visible

Women for Women International, led by Zainab Salbi, helps women survivors of war rebuild their lives and matches them with American women to provide personal connections and assistance (http://www.womenforwomen.org/).

Workforce studies of interest to women will be found at the website of the Families and Work Institute (http://www.familiesandwork.org/), led by Ellen Galinsky, who has also written a number of books on the topic. The best source for research on executive women is Catalyst (http://www.catalyst.org/).

Other resources to add to your list are Working Mother magazine and the book by its CEO and president, Carol Evans, This Is How We Do It: The Working Mother's Manifesto (New York: Hudson Street Press, 2006).

By far the best source for understanding the gender gap in voting is the Center for American Women in Politics, headed by Debbie Walsh (http://www .cawp.rutgers.edu/). An excellent resource related to single women is Women's Voices, Women Vote, headed by Page Gardner (http://www.wvwv.org/).

Chapter 8: Lifting as We Climb

Vital Voices Global Partnership, headed by President/CEO Alyse Nelson Bloom, has an excellent woman-to-woman mentoring model. The website is http:// www.vitalvoices.org/.

The National Partnership for Women and Families (http://www.national partnership.org/) is a very effective voice for women on Capitol Hill and is en-gaged in many campaigns, including the fight for paid family leave. It is headed by Debra Ness.

To learn more about women business owners and contracting, check out the National Association of Women Business Owners (http://www.nawbo.org/), which has a number of local chapters, and the Women's Business Enterprise National Council (http://www.wbenc.org/), led by Linda Denny.

Chapter 9: Wedging the Door Open

For information on the formal processes that other countries are using to see that more women are elected to office, see the UNIFEM website (http://www .unifem.org/) as well as Pamela Paxton and Melanie M. Hughes, Women, Politics and Power: A Global Perspective *(Thousand Oaks, CA: Pine Forge Press, 2007).*

To learn more about the UK and Norwegian experiences, take a look at the excellent presentations about women in the boardroom by executive coach Peninah Thomson on YouTube. Elin Hurvenes, an entrepreneur who founded the

Professional Boards Forum, has her own website at http://www.elinhurvenes .com/.

Chapter 10: Together, We Rise

More information on the Motherhood Manifesto can be found at http://www .momsrising.org/.

A comprehensive listing of women's organizations, many of which have local chapters, can be found on the website of the National Council of Women's Organizations, http://www.womensorganizations.org/.

Learn more about how you can participate in Emily's List at http://www.emilys list.org/.

There are two networks for women state legislators. The Women Legislators' Lobby (http://www.wand.org/will_home.htm), a program of Women Activists for New Directions, is headed by Georgia Representative Nan Orrock and Sue Shaer. The National Conference of State Legislatures has a Women's Legislative Network (http://www.ncsl.org/).

On family and medical leave, paid sick leave, and equal pay, take a look at the websites of the National Women's Law Center, headed by Marcia Greenberger and Duffy Campbell (http://www.nwlc.org/), and the National Partnership for Women and Families (http://www.nationalpartnership.org/). In addition, there is an excellent book by Evelyn Murphy with E. J. Graff, Getting Even: Why Women Don't Get Paid Like Men and What to Do about It *(New York: Touchstone, 2005).*

Numerous unions and women's organizations are involved in the equal pay effort, including NOW, AAUW, the Coalition of Labor Union Women, AFSCME, and the AFL-CIO.

Conclusion: Dreaming Bigger Dreams

See endnotes.

Acknowledgments

I owe a special debt of gratitude to the many people whose work has laid the groundwork for me and for you. Taking a journey like this means first standing on the shoulders of others who came before me to even see the lay of the land. You will find the work of many of them in the Resources. Then I've had special help along the way.

As a distinguished senior fellow at Demos, a network for ideas and action in New York City, I have had wonderful, strong support from the top down, starting with the president, Miles Rapoport—my friend and colleague for more than thirty years—the board of trustees, and the staff. Rachel Whiting has been both a colleague and my valued research associate. As a founder of Demos, I believe in the centrality of women's leadership to Demos's mission of increasing democratic participation and economic opportunity.

Numerous supporters have made it possible for me to put aside other things and work on this book for several years. I am enormously grateful to Ethel Klein and Ed Krugman; Gloria Steinem's Fund at the Ms. Foundation and its president, Sara Gould; the Chambers Family Fund and its president, Merle Chambers, and executive director, Letty Bass; and the W. K. Kellogg Foundation and the team of Karen Whalen, program director, and Anne Mosle, vice president and longtime colleague and friend. Without their financial support and personal encouragement this book would never have come to be.

From the beginning I've had a kitchen cabinet of special women who cheered me on when the going got tough. I thank especially Donna Hall, Kathy Bonk,

Donna Parson, and Ethel Klein for being there for me. I called on friends—old and new—to sit with me for interviews, network with their friends on my behalf, and arrange the twelve informal focus groups I held around the country to meet contemporary women and hear their views. All of the women who talked to me have informed this book. In Chicago I thank Sunny Fischer and Nancy Brand Boruch; in Washington my appreciation goes to Donna Klein, Virginia Littlejohn, Elizabeth Vazquez, Ritu Sharma, Esta Soler, Nora O'Connell, Anne Mosle, and Kathy Bonk; in Lexington, Kentucky, I am grateful to Janet Holloway; in New York City special thanks go to Joy Bunson, Diana Mason, and Rachel Whiting; in Fort Myers, Florida, our daughter, Melinda Walker, arranged the conversation; in Denver my thanks go to Letty Bass; and in Columbia, South Carolina, thank you to Linda Salane and Caroline Whitson.

My editor, Johanna Vondeling, the vice president for editorial and digital at Berrett-Koehler Publishers, has been a gem and a guru. Her wise counsel, thoughtful coaching, and unflagging interest in this project have made the book much better. The reviewers who read the drafts added a great deal, and I thank Gail Duwe, Linda Alepin, Shauna Shames, Donna Parson, and Kerry Radcliffe.

And now to the people closest to me who have seen me through the ups and downs of what turned out to be a far, far bigger endeavor than I ever imagined. A special thank you to our oldest granddaughter, Harper Jane Walker, who has been a cheerleader for the book ever since she knew I was writing a real "chapter book." And most of all, my love and appreciation go to Keith, my husband, partner, and the love of my life, with full knowledge that he has often only seen the back of my head as I sat at the computer and has never stopped encouraging me every step of the way.

Index

About the Author

Linda Tarr-Whelan is a premier expert on women's leadership in this country and internationally. As a frequent speaker to college and women's audiences, in the media, and as an advisor to top officials in the United States and Europe, Linda promotes more women in leadership as good business and smart politics. Her book, *Women Lead the Way: Your Guide to Stepping Up to Leadership and Changing the World*, brings her strong experience and personal convictions about women's strengths to the ground level with a practical road map for  women to move up. Currently a distinguished senior fellow at Demos, a network for ideas and action, she directs the Women's Leadership Initiative.

Ambassador Tarr-Whelan has always been a change agent. The constant thread in her life and work has been to lead beyond the status quo to a more egalitarian, peaceful, and just world. She has pursued the dream of women's advancement from her first day on the job as a nurse, when she was fired for failing to stand up when a doctor came into the room.

Linda's work as a nurse might seem a far cry from the rest of her illustrious career, but one that left a lifetime mark on her ability to listen and desire to reach out to help and empower others. It also taught her to endure eighteen-hour workdays, believe in the worth and dignity of individuals in the most menial as well as the most exalted of jobs, and encounter every kind of boss, from the empty suits and top-down autocrats to the most inclusive and collaborative. When frozen systems didn't budge, she helped to create or build organizations to make them move, including the Center for Women in Government, the Coalition of Labor Union Women, the Center for Policy Alternatives, Demos, and Quantum Leaps, Inc. Linda was a U.S. delegate to the groundbreaking UN Fourth World Conference on the Status of Women in Beijing, and her career path and networks stretch across the globe.

She and her husband, Keith, created their own consulting firm, Tarr-Whelan & Associates, Inc., advising small and large national and international organizations on managing change, but she got there after a career of commitment to the ideal that women should play a central and key leadership role in organizations, government, and politics. She lived and worked in leadership roles in all those worlds—as a union organizer and negotiator; as the lead lobbyist for a two-million-member teachers' organization; as a deputy assistant to President Jimmy Carter in the White House when she was thirty-nine; as the administrative director of a large state agency in New York; as the head of a nationally recognized policy and leadership development organization, the Center for Policy Alternatives; and as a U.S. ambassador to the UN Commission on the Status of Women, appointed by President Bill Clinton—all positions that have traditionally been the preserve of men. At every stop along the way she has brought other women in and up.

Through all this she has placed her family and their well-being first, balancing both, just like most women. Linda is a survivor of colon cancer. She and her husband, Keith, have been true partners on this journey, together with their two children, Melinda Walker and Scott Tarr-Whelan, and their four grandchildren. The couple lives on St. Helena Island, South Carolina.

Linda graduated from the Johns Hopkins Hospital School of Nursing and has a BSN from Johns Hopkins University, an MS from the University of Maryland, and honorary PhDs from Chatham University and Plymouth State University. She is a fellow of the American Academy of Nursing, has been honored for her leadership by numerous universities and organizations, and has served on dozens of boards of directors at the community, state, and national levels. She currently chairs the National Women's Advisory Council for Pax World, which includes the Women's Equity Fund, and is a cochair of the Leadership Circle for the effort to ratify CEDAW, the Women's Treaty, as well as having an active role in her church, the Unitarian Universalist Fellowship of Beaufort, South Carolina, and serving on the board of the Child Abuse Prevention Association of Port Royal, South Carolina.

Dēmos

Dēmos is a non-partisan, public policy, research and advocacy organization founded in 2000. Headquartered in New York City, Dēmos works with advocates and policy-makers around the country in pursuit of four overarching goals:

- a more equitable economy with widely shared prosperity and opportunity;
- a vibrant and inclusive democracy with high levels of voting and civic engagement;
- an empowered public sector that works for the common good;
- and responsible U.S. engagement in an interdependent world.

WOMEN'S LEADERSHIP INITIATIVE

Despite enormous progress over the past several decades in this country, as well as the historic nomination of a woman presidential and vice-presidential candidate in the 2008 election, the facts are clear: American women are the majority of voters, 80 percent of consumers, the majority of graduates of colleges, professional and graduate programs, and the driving force of entrepreneurship. And yet the wage gap persists, only a handful of women are on corporate boards or in corner offices—no matter the field or profession, women business owners still face unnecessary obstacles, Congress is only 16 percent women, and quality affordable and accessible childcare—concerns that most affect mothers—are still only a dream for most. A deeper conversation must enter the public debate about women's extremely poor numbers in top leadership positions compared to the rest of the world -whether access to the top is still not readily available to women, and what realities exist that force women to choose not to lead or constrain their options as leaders.

The Women's Leadership Initiative, a multi-year project of Demos led by Distinguished Senior Fellow Linda Tarr-Whelan (WLI), provides a platform for this conversation and a vehicle for entrance into the public debate. The WLI will open this space in the public debate through a series of public events, a new book by Linda Tarr-Whelan, reports and a media campaign.

About Berrett-Koehler Publishers

Berrett-Koehler is an independent publisher dedicated to an ambitious mission: Creating a World That Works for All.

We believe that to truly create a better world, action is needed at all levels—individual, organizational, and societal. At the individual level, our publications help people align their lives with their values and with their aspirations for a better world. At the organizational level, our publications promote progressive leadership and management practices, socially responsible approaches to business, and humane and effective organizations. At the societal level, our publications advance social and economic justice, shared prosperity, sustainability, and new solutions to national and global issues.

A major theme of our publications is "Opening Up New Space." They challenge conventional thinking, introduce new ideas, and foster positive change. Their common quest is changing the underlying beliefs, mindsets, and structures that keep generating the same cycles of problems, no matter who our leaders are or what improvement programs we adopt.

We strive to practice what we preach—to operate our publishing company in line with the ideas in our books. At the core of our approach is *stewardship*, which we define as a deep sense of responsibility to administer the company for the benefit of all of our "stakeholder" groups: authors, customers, employees, investors, service providers, and the communities and environment around us.

We are grateful to the thousands of readers, authors, and other friends of the company who consider themselves to be part of the "BK Community." We hope that you, too, will join us in our mission.

A BK Currents Book

This book is part of our BK Currents series. BK Currents books advance social and economic justice by exploring the critical intersections between business and society. Offering a unique combination of thoughtful analysis and progressive alternatives, BK Currents books promote positive change at the national and global levels. To find out more, visit www.bkcurrents.com.

Be Connected

Visit Our Website

Go to www.bkconnection.com to read exclusive previews and excerpts of new books, find detailed information on all Berrett-Koehler titles and authors, browse subject-area libraries of books, and get special discounts.

Subscribe to Our Free E-Newsletter

Be the first to hear about new publications, special discount offers, exclusive articles, news about bestsellers, and more! Get on the list for our free e-newsletter by going to www.bkconnection.com.

Get Quantity Discounts

Berrett-Koehler books are available at quantity discounts for orders of ten or more copies. Please call us toll-free at (800) 929-2929 or email us at bkp.orders@aidcvt.com.

Host a Reading Group

For tips on how to form and carry on a book reading group in your workplace or community, see our website at www.bkconnection.com.

Join the BK Community

Thousands of readers of our books have become part of the "BK Community" by participating in events featuring our authors, reviewing draft manuscripts of forthcoming books, spreading the word about their favorite books, and supporting our publishing program in other ways. If you would like to join the BK Community, please contact us at bkcommunity@bkpub.com.